IMAGES
of America

KA'U DISTRICT

IMAGES
of America

KA'U DISTRICT

Dennis and Marge Elwell
Foreword by Cindy Orlando

ARCADIA
PUBLISHING

Published by Arcadia Publishing
Charleston, South Carolina

Library of Congress Control Number: 2014957992 .

For all general information, please contact Arcadia Publishing:
Telephone 843-853-2070
Fax 843-853-0044
E-mail sales@arcadiapublishing.com
For customer service and orders:
Toll-Free 1-888-313-2665

Visit us on the Internet at www.arcadiapublishing.com

*Dedicated to the late Emmett Cahill, who inspired us
to work on local history in our retirement years*

CONTENTS

FOREWORD

Being asked to write this foreword is bittersweet for me. Though I grew up on Oʻahu and left after my first year at Manoa, I had spent little time on Hawaiʻi Island and first visited Kaʻu in the late 1990s. I have vivid memories of driving down the hill into Waiohinu and happening upon the AlohaFest event in Waiohinu Park. I was so impressed—the island traditions and customs were shared in such a way that I knew if I ever returned and lived anywhere on this island it would be in Kaʻu. Unbeknownst to me at the time, that would happen in 2004. Today, I call Kaʻu my home.

Sometimes, we forget how incredibly fortunate we are to live here. The remarkable convergence of culture, geology, biology, history, and numerous other factors enhancing our quality of life contributes to all that is unique about Kaʻu and its rich heritage. As a gateway to Hawaiʻi Volcanoes National Park, we share our two volcanoes, Mauna Loa and Kilauea, with our sister Puna. As part of a larger island community, we embrace the aloha spirit of Hawaiʻi Island and send that message to the world. With this publication, we celebrate the pictorial history of our special place and the passion of the authors, Marge and Dennis Elwell. We mahalo all of you, and our visitors to the area, for being a part of its preservation.

—Cindy Orlando
Superintendent, Hawaiʻi Volcanoes National Park

ACKNOWLEDGMENTS

We are grateful to the many people who have made this book possible.

Assembling a collection of around 200 photographs to give an overview of the history of Ka'u District was a challenging task, and we wish to thank all those who helped us put together the collection that forms the core of this book. We rely especially on the archives of museums and other organizations and the dedicated staff who collect and organize the collections of photographs that are donated or collected over the years. Special thanks go to Laura Schuster and Kristi Ausfresser at Hawai'i Volcanoes National Park, who provided among other inspiring photographs the one that became our cover image. Miki Bulos of the Lyman Museum Archives was particularly helpful and kind enough to waive use fees, an important contribution to our budget. Hawai'i State Archives are the best source of historical photographs in the state, and we thank the staff and volunteers who have been digitizing and organizing the collection. We had the privilege to work with respected Honolulu photographer Franco Salmoiraghi on our *History of Pahala* and appreciate his consent to use those photographs in this book.

We also thank talented local photographers Peter Anderson and Bill Doar for permission to include black-and-white versions of a few of their photographs. Mahalo, Walter Wong Yuen, for an excellent job of assembling a collection of local photographs at Pahala County Library, and Sandy Sinclair, great-nephew of sugar pioneer C.N. Spencer, for photographs from his personal collection. We also wish to thank the following: Jim O'Hara, Laura Foster and Sydney Sampson for photographs of Ocean View, Ric Elhard for photographs of Kula Kai Caverns, and Iwao Yonemitsu and the late Jean Cooper for Na'alehu photographs. The sources of other photographs are acknowledged in the text.

Thank you, Rita Pregana, Iwao Yonemitsu, and Debbie Wong Yuen, for thoughtful reviews of our draft.

INTRODUCTION

The Ka'u District is the southernmost in the state and therefore in the United States, except for territories. It is also the largest district in Hawai'i at 922 square miles. Ka'u is located on the southern slopes of Mauna Loa, the world's largest mountain, as measured from its base on the ocean floor. Since Mauna Loa and its neighbor Kilauea are very active volcanoes, some part of Ka'u is on rather recent lava, which is unsuitable for agriculture. The alternation of old and new lava and the rather quirky rainfall pattern means that visually Ka'u has a landscape of contrasts, with stark lava fields interspersed with green, dry forest. Its scenic appeal is based on this variety, together with the mountain and ocean views.

The meaning of the name Ka'u is controversial. The authoritative *Place Names of Hawai'i* by Mary Kawena Pukui just notes that the name is ancient and used elsewhere in the South Pacific. A dictionary definition lists "mine," which suggests that the name was used to indicate that Ka'u is the possession of the volcano goddess Pele. An alternative meaning is that the word was used for "breast" and suggested by the gently sloping shape of the shield volcano Mauna Loa.

Historically, Ka'u has a strong claim as the location of the first landings by the Polynesian voyagers who were the first inhabitants and came from the south. There are several harbors suitable for landing oceangoing canoes and strong archaeological evidence of early occupation, from around the 3rd or 4th century CE. In chapter 1, we discuss the evidence that the first landing and occupation of Hawai'i was in the area around Ka Lae, South Point. The Pu'u Ali'i sand dune was the site where Kenneth Emory and coworkers pioneered the use of modern archaeological techniques in Hawai'i; in most locations, the lava rock or rocky soil does not lend itself to systematic layer-by-layer excavation. Pu'u Ali'i yielded over 1,000 fishhooks that provided the evidence for the first occupation and the conclusion that the first arrivals in Hawai'i came from the Marquesas. The South Point area is not the most favorable for settlement since it is dry and windswept, but the waters offshore are excellent fishing grounds, so it is no coincidence that the artifacts from the first occupation are rich in fishhooks.

In the late 19th century, as the ali'i battled for control of the island, Ka'u's last chief, Keoua Ku'ahu'ula, and his warriors were never conquered and gained for Ka'u a reputation for their ferocity. After almost a decade of fighting, Keoua agreed to attend a truce meeting with Kamehameha but was killed there, paving the way for Kamehameha to become king of a united Hawai'i. One theory of why Keoua agreed to the truce is that many of his warriors were killed in an unusual eruption of the Kilauea volcano, in which noxious gases were emitted in fatal concentration. Keoua may have interpreted this event as a sign that the volcano goddess was displeased with him. Evidence for the fatal eruption of Kilauea can be seen at the Footprints Trail in Hawai'i Volcanoes National Park. Since the eruption also brought ash in a time of rain, footprints of the ancient warriors can be seen preserved as patterns in the solidified mud.

Waiohinu was a location that was favored by Ka'u's ali'i, since it has moderate rainfall, is sheltered from the trade winds, and was supplied with water from the historically famous Ha'ao Spring. In 1819, the missionary William Ellis saw sugarcane, bananas, and dry taro being cultivated near Waiohinu, and his impression of abundant agriculture was confirmed by Mark Twain in 1866. Twain planted a monkeypod tree, a descendant of which is signposted along the highway.

The first missionary to Ka'u was Catholic—Fr. Joachim Mareschal, who arrived in 1841 but met some opposition and had to retreat to the village of Ho'opuloa, just north of Miloli'i. He returned in 1842 and established a presence in Hilea, just before the arrival in Ka'u of the first Protestant missionary, Rev. John D. Paris. Reverend Paris built his church in Waiohinu, and Father Mareschal was reassigned and replaced by Fr. Agathange Grould, who built his church in nearby Na'ohule'elua ("two bald men"). Relations between Catholic and Protestant missionaries were often acrimonious, as in other parts of Hawai'i. The Catholic missionaries belonged to the Sacred Heart Fathers, of France and Belgium, and their group included Fr. Damien de Veuster, who was later to become famous, and eventually canonized, for his work at the Hansen's disease settlement of Kalaupapa on Moloka'i. De Veuster was among the itinerant group of priests who traveled miles on horseback with a ministry that included Ka'u District.

Agriculture has been historically the main economic activity in Ka'u, especially sugarcane. A key factor in the growth of the industry was the Great Mahele of 1848, which allowed non-Hawaiians to buy land. John Costa, an Italian, and Alexander Hutchinson were pioneers of sugar plantation and mill investment in Ka'u from about 1868. The Hawaiian Agricultural Company incorporated in 1876 and was the largest in Hawai'i. Mills built in Na'alehu and Pahala in the late 1800s for processing cane into sugar were among the largest in the world. Wharves were built at Honu'apo and Punalu'u, and cane was transported by mules, flumes, and later rail and trucks. The industry flourished until foreign competition forced a decline, and in 1996 the last sugar mill closed in Pahala. Ranching was the second-most important economic activity and continues today, although on a reduced scale and under pressure to remain viable.

The sugar industry in particular led to a need for imported labor, and the plantation owners in the late 19th century began bringing laborers from rural areas around the world, notably from China, Portugal, Japan, Korea, and the Philippines. A census in 1884 reported that the labor population in Ka'u included 1,543 Hawaiians and part-Hawaiians, 568 Chinese, and 933 Portuguese. The total population of Ka'u was around 6,000, not much lower than it is today. Workers were housed in camps built by the plantation owners, often for a single ethnic group, like Korean Camp and Moaula Filipino Camp. Since many workers stayed after their initial contracts expired, the sugar industry was the main origin of the racial mixture that exists in Ka'u today, especially when retirees from the mainland are added to the mix. The immigrants brought with them their homeland religions, so Ka'u also has a large variety of churches and temples for its fairly sparse population. For example, there are Jodo Shinsu temples in Na'alehu and Pahala, a Tibetan Buddhist temple in Wood Valley, and Iglesia ni Cristo and Assembly of God churches.

There has not been any single major economic activity to replace the sugar plantations, but Ka'u coffee is building an excellent reputation and winning both statewide and international competitions. It has some way to go before it rivals Kona coffee in volume, but the foundations have been laid, and the Ka'u Coffee Festival is now the largest annual event in the district. Ka'u offers several opportunities to visit a working coffee farm, where traditional practices are used to make a true gourmet coffee. The Na'alehu rodeo continues a tradition that began when cattle ranching was flourishing. Macadamia nuts are also an important component of Ka'u's agricultural economy.

Socially, Ka'u is of interest as the domain of the study for *The Polynesian Family System in Ka'u* by Mary Kawena Pukui and E.S. Craighill Handy. The book optimistically predicts, "It seems probable that in this thriving green heartland of tumultuous Ka'u will long remain Kane's primordial domain and, whether in sugarcane or some subsequent economy, will continue to contribute bounteously to the well-being of man."

The presence of the volcanoes has a positive impact on the region; Ka'u is the home of the Hawai'i Volcanoes National Park, perhaps the most important tourist attraction in the state. In 2003, the park added the Kahuku unit, one of very few recent additions to the national park system. Much of Ka'u lies between the two units of the national park. Thanks to the action of the Kilauea volcano, visitors often have the chance to witness the growth of new land. Highlights of the national park include the Crater Rim Drive that circles the Kilauea Summit caldera and passes through rain forest and stark lava, with stops along the way. The Chain of Craters Road is a 36-mile round-trip that descends from 3,700 feet elevation to the coast, passing an extensive field of petroglyphs and ending where the road is closed by a lava flow.

In addition to the national park, Kaʻu has the asset of a relatively untouched and scenic coastline, and there has been some support in Congress for the Kaʻu coastline to become a national seashore. Kaʻu has some of the largest stretches of relatively untouched landscape and coastline anywhere in the state, and the absence of development in Kaʻu could become its greatest asset. Punaluʻu Beach Park has one of the best-known black sand beaches in the state and is home of the *honu*, the Hawaiian green sea turtle.

Already, the state highway in Kaʻu has been designated a Hawaiʻi State Scenic Byway, and there are plans for the Ala Kahakai National Historic Trail, a hiking trail circling around most of the island near the shoreline, including the whole of Kaʻu. Kaʻu could become a magnet for ecotourists and those who appreciate its natural beauty, as the basis of a new prosperity that conserves and treasures the best of its natural resources.

One

THE DISCOVERY OF HAWAI'I AND FISHHOOKS REVELATIONS

The ancient Polynesians recorded their history not on paper but in chants, but no chant has survived that tells the name of the navigator who led the first oceangoing canoe to discover the most remote island group on the planet.

The voyagers came from the south, so it would not be a surprise if the first landing in the Hawaiian Islands was at the southernmost tip, Ka Lae (South Point). The area is dry and windswept but has access to excellent fishing, both in the shallows and in the deeper water beyond. It is no coincidence that the dominant artifacts found in excavations nearby are fishhooks.

Support for the idea that the first Hawaiian settlements were in the South Point area comes from archaeology. Kenneth Emory, with his team of William Bonk and Yoshiko Sinoto, came up with a date of approximately 290 CE for the earliest artifacts found in a site there called Pu'u Ali'i.

Sinoto in particular made a detailed study of fishhook styles and developed a chronology of fishhook change based on their large collection from the South Point area. The Emory team concluded that the earliest forms were close in design to those found in the Marquesas, and this reinforced linguistic studies showing that the Hawaiian language is more similar to Marqesan than Tahitian. Changes in fishhook design could have been influenced by the later arrival of greater numbers from Tahiti and its neighbor islands, which eventually became the dominant group.

Ka'u District played an important role in the struggle for the formation of a single Hawaiian kingdom. Some of the last battles between the last ali'i (chief) of Ka'u, Keoua Ku'ahu'ula, and Kamehameha's general Ka'iana were fought in that neighborhood. There were at least three battles just inland from South Point, with Ka'iana having the upper hand. Keoua retreated to Puna and was the winner in the clashes there, and Ka'iana retreated to his canoes. After a decade of fighting for control of the island, Keoua apparently went willingly to his death at the new heiau (temple) of Pu'ukohola. Having gained control of Hawai'i Island, it became much easier for Kamehameha to become the king of a united Hawai'i.

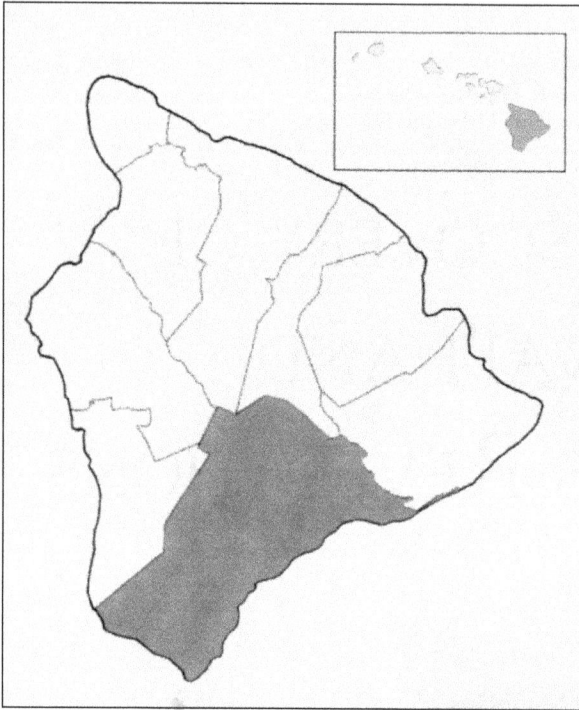

Ka'u District (shaded) is the southernmost in Hawai'i and therefore in the 50 states. It is also the largest in the state; at 922 square miles, it is larger than O'ahu, Moloka'i, and Kaho'olawe combined. Ka'u sits on the southern slopes of Mauna Loa, an active volcano and the largest mountain mass in the world as measured from its base deep in the Pacific Ocean. Most of the Hawai'i Volcanoes National Park, including the entire Kahuku unit, is located in Ka'u District. The insert shows the state of Hawai'i, with Hawai'i County shaded. (Hawai'i County Planning Department.)

Polynesian voyagers using double-hulled canoes began to explore the Pacific Ocean almost 2,000 years ago. The canoes were very well designed and built and have been called "the greatest achievement of ancient Polynesia." The amazing achievement includes navigation over long-range voyages without compass, sextant, or chart. Some oceangoing canoes could hold 100 people and were capable of speeds over 10 knots. (Hawai'i Nei.)

The Pu'u Ali'i sand dune was the site of over 14,000 artifacts recovered in the 1950s by Kenneth Emory and coworkers. The excavations unearthed 1,710 fishhooks and tools used in their manufacture. (Authors' collection.)

The Pu'u Ali'i site was labeled H1 and is located just to the east of the tip of Ka Lae (South Point). The east side has more easy landing sites than the west, where there are tall and scenic cliffs extending to the Kahuku Pali and the former village of Wai'Ahukini. (*Feathered Gods and Fishhooks.*)

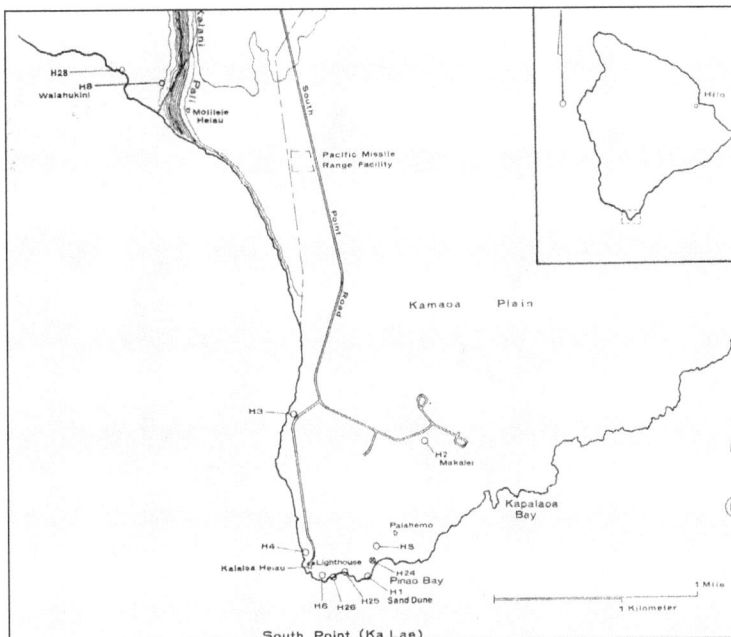

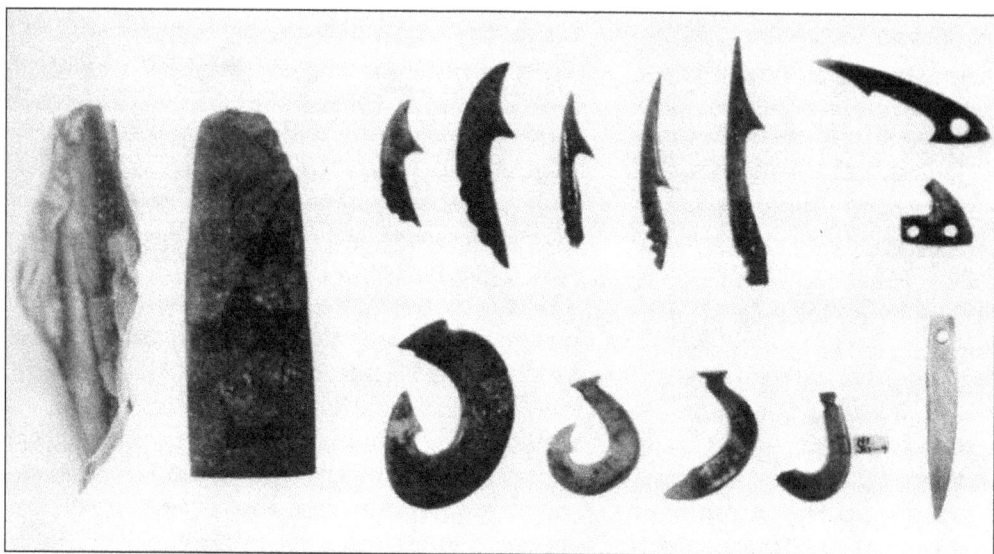

The fishhooks from Pu'u Ali'i were found to be of various styles, some made in a single piece and some in two pieces to be tied together. Emory and Sinoto concluded that the older fishhooks were of a design originating in the Marquesas, and the later fishhooks were in a style associated with the islands around Tahiti. The artifacts on the left are examples of tools used to make the fishhooks. (*Feathered Gods and Fishhooks.*)

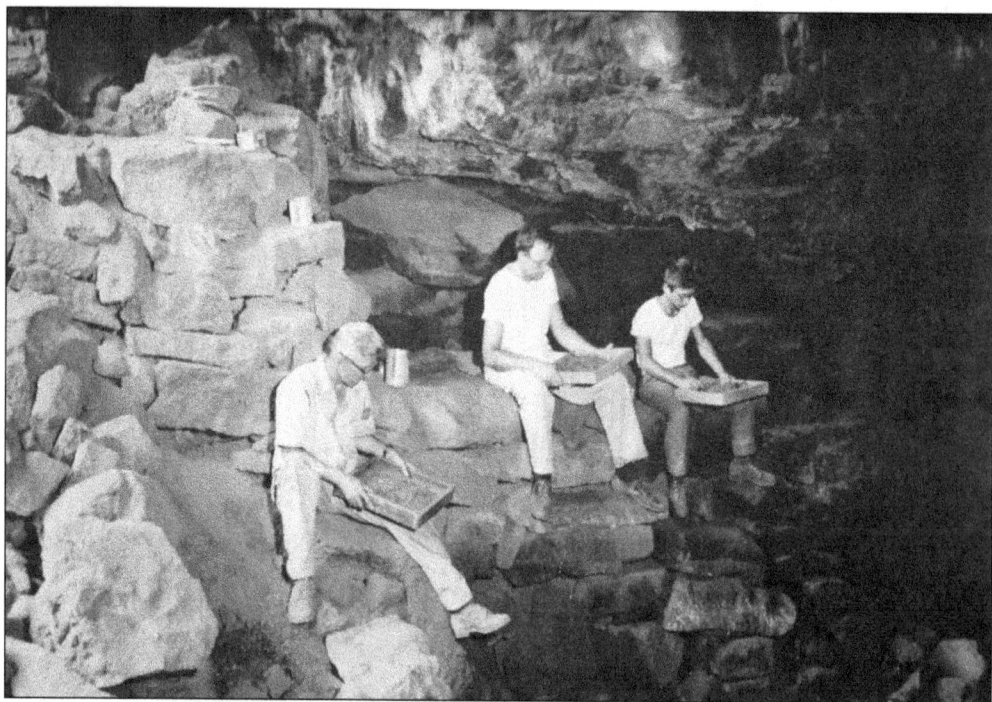

Kenneth Emory (left), William Bonk (center), and Yoshiko Sinoto are pictured here sifting material in 1955 at Makalei Shelter Cave, labeled H2 on the map of the South Point area. Artifacts from the Makalei cave were of much later origin than those from Pu'u Ali'i, from the 16th to the 18th centuries. ("Historical Background of the South Point Area, Ka'u, Hawai'i.")

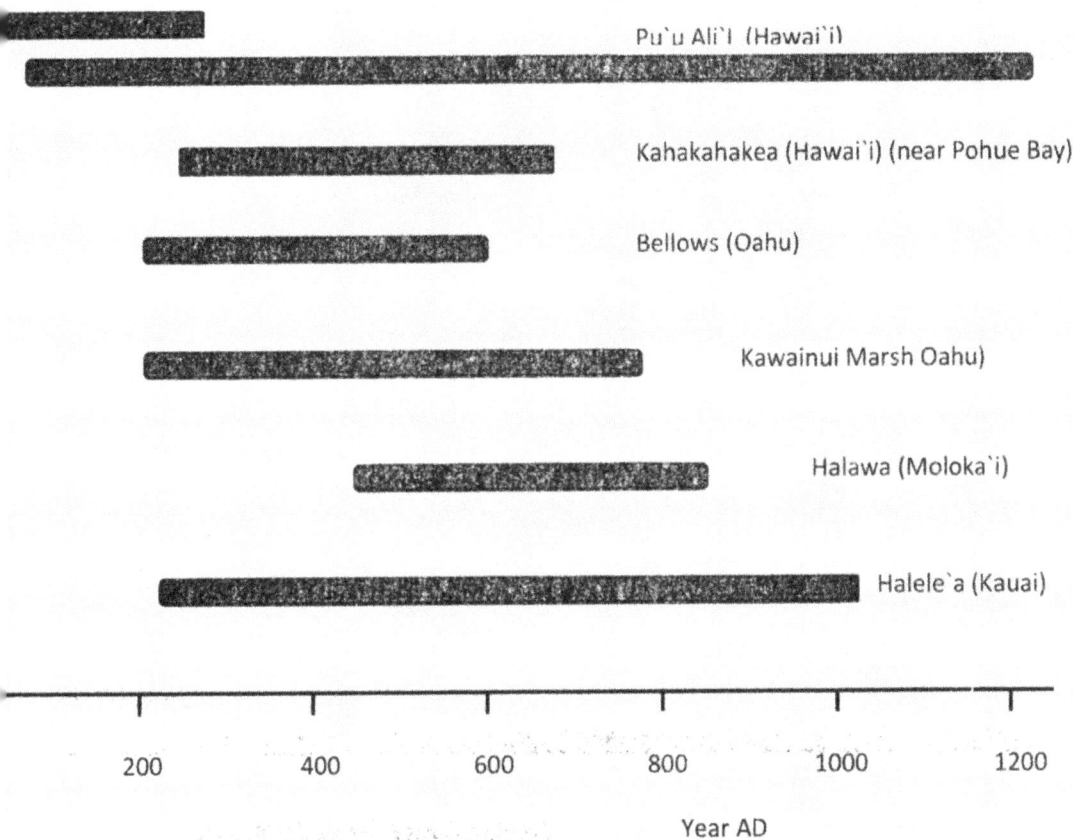

Pu`u Ali`I (Hawai`i)

Kahakahakea (Hawai`i) (near Pohue Bay)

Bellows (Oahu)

Kawainui Marsh Oahu)

Halawa (Moloka`i)

Halele`a (Kauai)

200	400	600	800	1000	1200

Year AD

This is a radiocarbon dating of the ages of the earliest artifacts found in different locations in Hawai'i. Radiocarbon dates are normally considered to be about 95 percent reliable, but this assumes that the samples are uncontaminated, so disputes among scholars are common. The Pu'u Ali'i site has the earliest dates shown, but many scholars dispute dates before about 300 CE. The results do show that artifacts dated at around 400 CE were found at several sites around Hawai'i, and there appears to have been continuous occupation from then on. For a later critical review of radiocarbon data, see chapter 4 of *Exalted Sits the Chief* by Ross Cordy.

15

There are many mooring holes in the South Point area. Fishermen used to tie their canoes to one of the holes so that they had two hands free for fishing in the treacherous waters around the point. (Authors' collection.)

Salt pans were carved into the lava rock and seawater allowed to evaporate to yield salt. Before refrigeration, salt was particularly valuable for the preservation of food. (Authors' collection.)

Above is a corner of the Kalalea heiau at South Point. The heiau was dedicated to Ku'ula, the principal god of fishermen. (Authors' collection.)

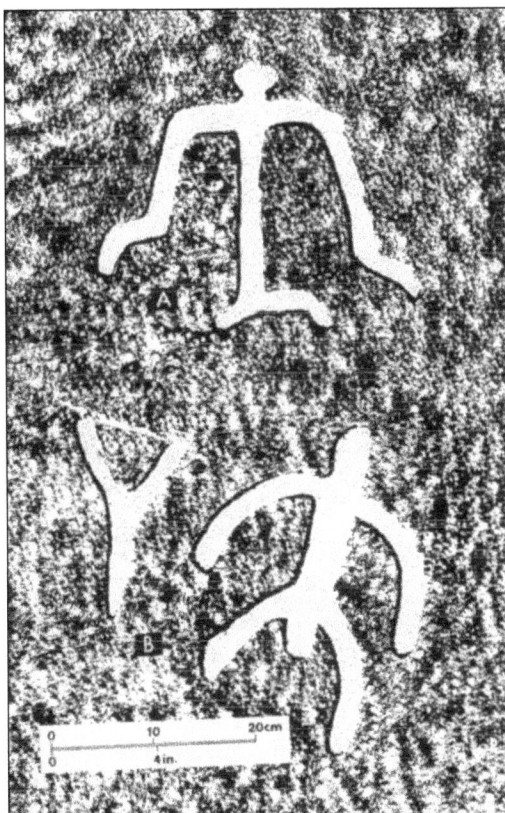

These petroglyphs were the only ones found at South Point. Many more are located in Pohue Bay to the northwest, still in Ka'u District, one of the most important petroglyph sites in Hawai'i. ("Archaeological and Historic Survey of Pakini-nui and Pakini-iki Coastal Sites.")

Shown here is a view of the impressive scarp that runs along the Kahuku Fault, along the southwest rift zone of Mauna Loa. The 1868 lava flow is the black zone at the foot of the *pali* (cliff). Just below the cliff at the water's edge there are traces of the former village of Wai'Ahukini, the principal home of Chief Kalaniopu'u. (Authors' collection.)

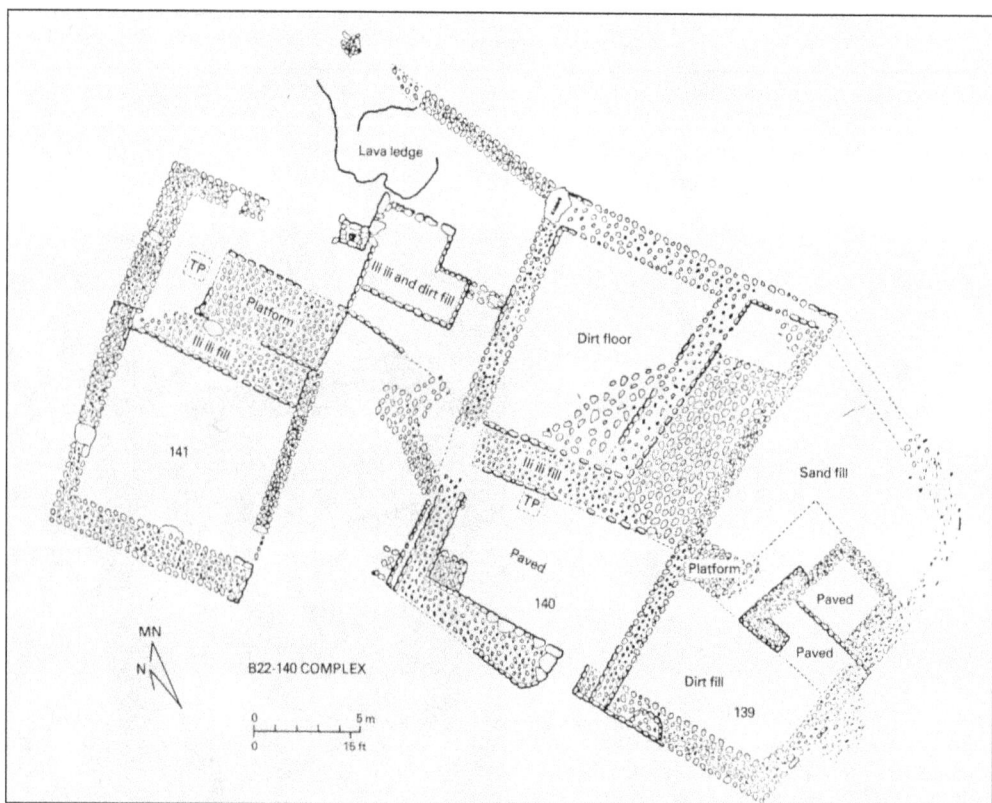

Shown is the layout of the chief's complex in Wai'Ahukini, from the 1973 excavations of Sinoto and Kelly. This was presumably the dwelling of Kalaniopu'u when he was at the site. ("Archaeological and Historic Survey of Pakini-nui and Pakini-iki Coastal Sites.")

Kalaniopu'u, the high chief of Hawai'i Island, greeted Captain Cook on his arrival in 1778. When Kalaniopu'u died in 1782, the ali'i quarreled over the division of the island's lands, and fighting soon began. Kalaniopu'u's son and heir, Kiwala'o, was killed in one of the early skirmishes, so the conflict began between Kamehameha and his cousin Keoua. (Illustration by John Webber, R.A.)

Depicted here is Keoua Ku'ahu'ula, ali'i of Ka'u. Keoua fought for almost a decade with his cousin Kamehameha for control of Hawai'i Island, with Kamehameha controlling the north and west and Keoua the south and east of the island. In the last campaign in 1790, Kamehameha sent his general Ka'iana, who landed his canoes near South Point, and battles were fought, according to the historian Abraham Fornander, at Paiaha'a, Kama'oa, and Ua'ohulelua. Ka'iana had the better of the fighting, especially at the latter site, and Keoua retreated to Puna District. There, he regrouped and had the upper hand, capturing some of Ka'iana's European weapons, so Ka'iana retreated to his canoes. (Sketch by Dennis Elwell, based on the video *Ho'oku'ikahi* by Meleanna Aluli Meyer.)

After almost a decade of fighting, Kamehameha changed his tactics and built the great heiau of Pu'ukohola, then invited Keoua to a truce meeting there. Keoua went, knowing that the heiau required a noble sacrifice, and that he was probably going there to die. According to historian Samuel Kamakau, on the way to the meeting, he went ashore and cut off his penis, a gesture to degrade the sacrifice of his body to Kamehameha's war god. As he approached the landing site, Keoua and many of his followers were killed. (*Pele: Goddess of Hawaii's Volcanoes.*)

After Keoua's death, Kamehameha assumed control over Hawai'i Island, and, with his base secured, it was then relatively easy for him to complete the conquest of the other islands and become the first king of all Hawai'i. (Authors' collection.)

KAMEHAMEHA THE GREAT

Two

SUGAR, PLANTATIONS, AND POPULATION CHANGE

The growth of the sugar plantations in Hawai'i led to the largest change in population demographics since the first inhabitants. The sugar industry is labor-intensive, and there were not enough Native Hawaiians willing to exchange their lifestyle for hard work in the fields or the mills for low pay. As the industry grew in the late 19th century, the plantation owners were forced to look around the world for agricultural workers prepared to travel to Hawai'i, normally on contracts that paid their passage and provided benefits in exchange for a commitment to work a certain number of years. China, Portugal, Japan, the Philippines, and Korea provided the majority of sugar workers, as the industry grew to become the dominant source of commerce. According to unofficial census data, Native Hawaiians accounted for 97 percent of the population in 1850 but only 33 percent by 1890. There was much intermarriage, and many immigrant workers decided to stay rather than return home after their contracts expired.

In Ka'u District, the plantations and mills sprang up rapidly. The first mill was built by Nicholas George in Waiohinu in 1866 (see chapter 5), processing sugarcane from a number of small enterprises. In that area, Alexander Hutchinson became the dominant figure. Together with John Costa, he built a large mill in Na'alehu and consolidated operations until his death in 1879 in an accident while he was chasing two runaway contract workers. In 1870, Charles Spencer, William Irwin, and Hutchinson built a mill in Hilea, then Irwin and Claus Spreckels bought the Na'alehu Sugar Company from the Hutchinson estate and incorporated as Hutchinson Sugar Company. Honu'apo was established as the harbor for Ka'u sugar, and the last of several mills was built there. Over the same time period, a group of bankers, including Charles Bishop, John Dominis, and Peter Jones, leased acreage around Pahala and built the most modern mill in the district there in 1880. The Hawaiian Agricultural Company grew by mergers and changed its name to Ka'u Sugar Company in 1972 and to Ka'u Agribusiness Company in 1986 as it diversified into macadamia nuts. Economic pressures on the whole Hawaiian sugar industry grew, and Ka'u Agribusiness became the last survivor, but the plantation and mill closed in 1996.

Charles N. Spencer (left) was one of the founders of the mill at Hilea. On the right is a Mr. McIntosh, believed to be the manager of the mill, with his daughter. (Sandy Sinclair.)

Shown here is a typical sugar mill, the Hilea Mill, built by Charles Spencer, Alexander Hutchinson, John Smith Walker, and William G. Irwin in 1877. Hutchinson was a prominent pioneer of the sugar industry, but he was killed in a boating accident in 1879 while chasing workers who were fleeing to escape the terms of their contract. (Hawai'i State Archives.)

Some sugarcane was cut into pieces 12 inches or more in length for use as seeds. It was planted by hand in rows 20 to 24 inches deep then covered with a few inches of soil. The photograph shows sacks of seed cane being hauled by mules to the fields for planting. (Hawaiian Sugar Planters Association.)

Workers are shown here cutting cane. The hats suggest that the workers are Chinese immigrants. Manual cutting was the preferred method of cutting cane through most of its history in Hawai'i, although machines were used in the later years. (Hawai'i State Archives.)

Pictured here is cane being transported on carts pulled by oxen. This photograph is dated around 1887. (Hawai'i State Archives.)

This worker seems to be carrying a ton of cane. A more careful look shows that most of the cane in the photograph is on a cart behind him. However, the photograph does illustrate how sugar growing put heavy demands on the field-workers. (Lyman Museum.)

A *luna*, or overseer, inspects the cane fields from the top of a ladder. A horse was his normal transport around the plantation. (Hawai'i State Archives.)

Mules were used in the early years as versatile carriers in the fields or from the field to the mill. This mule is pulling a cart on rails, a precursor to trains, which later became the preferred method of transport to the mills, replacing animals and flumes. (Mission Houses Museum Library.)

A popular early method of transporting the cut cane to the mills was in flumes, V-shaped wooden troughs laid from the fields with water used as the transport medium and gravity providing the force needed for the cane to flow. Here, women watch the cane arrive at the end of a flume near the Pahala Mill. (Lyman Museum.)

One problem with fluming was that the cane could mesh together and jam up the flow. Here, a watchman is sitting on his perch watching for flume jams around 1925. (Pahala Library.)

Trains were sometimes run on movable lines right into the cane fields. This photograph of an early train is from Waimanalo on Oʻahu. (Hawaiʻi State Archives.)

This is the engine *Kilauea*, which was used to haul sugarcane for the Hutchinson Sugar Company. (Hawaiʻi State Archives.)

Shown here is the rail terminus in Pahala, where the trains could be turned around on a turntable. This photograph was likely taken in the 1930s. (*Hawai'i Statehood Edition.*)

Pictured here is a crane picking up cane in the field for loading onto flumes or trucks. (Franco Salmoiraghi.)

Eventually, trucks became the preferred method of transportation to the mills, as they could also be used to take the sugar to the ports to be shipped for refining, usually in California. (Franco Salmoiraghi.)

This is a long line of trucks working for the Ka'u Sugar Company, probably in the 1940s. The number of trucks is an indication of how popular trucking had become. (Pahala Library.)

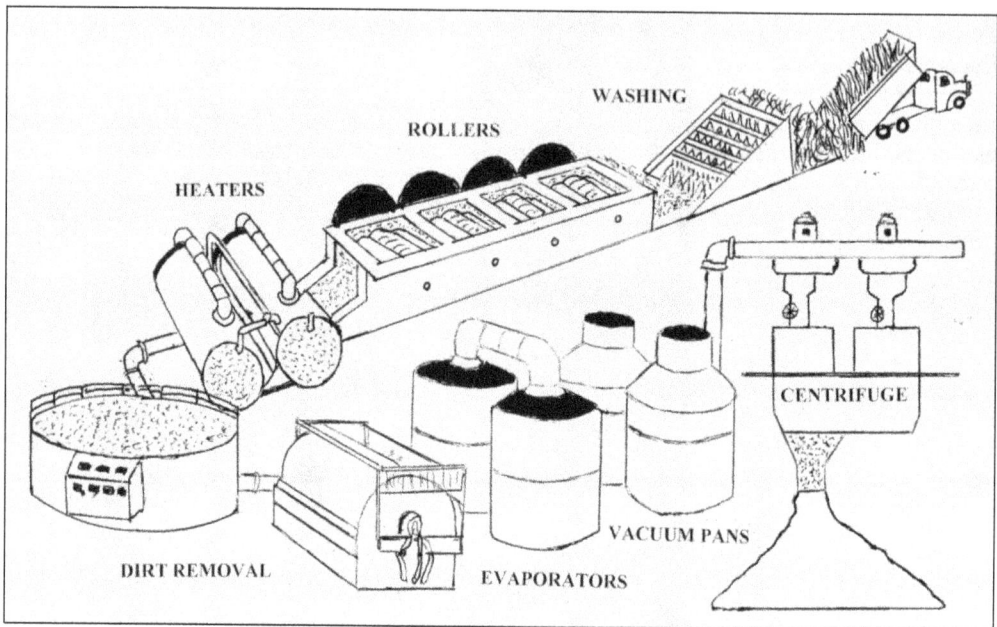

This is a schematic of the process steps in an older mill to convert cane into sugar. (Authors' collection.)

This artist's impression depicts the interior of an early sugar mill. The wheels on some steam engines were twice the height of a man. (Hawaiian Sugar Planters Association.)

Shown here is the interior of the Pahala Mill at night. The Hawaiian Agricultural Company was formed in 1876 by a high-powered group, including banker Charles Bishop; John Dominis, the husband of future queen Lydia Lili'uokalani; and Peter Jones Jr., who later became president of C. Brewer and Company, the company's agents and future owners. Soon, the mill was turning out 45,000 tons of sugar per year and became the star performer of the sugar industry in Ka'u, the last mill to close down, in 1996. (Franco Salmoiraghi.)

Chinese men are pictured here arriving in Honolulu in 1901 on the SS *America Maru*. Passage was paid in return for a commitment to work three to five years on the plantations. Workers were paid only $3 a month but received "good and sufficient food and comfortable house room." (Hawai'i State Archives.)

A line of Japanese field-workers leaves a ship, carrying their belongings along the so-called immigration bridge. Most expected to save their earnings and return to Japan, but pay was poor and many decided to stay in Hawai'i at the end of their contracts. (Hawai'i State Archives.)

Women field-workers pose in front of the cane, probably in the 1890s. (Hawai'i State Archives.)

Many women came as picture brides, sent from Japan to meet their husbands who had chosen them based on photographs. But they still had to work. This group of picture brides is shown with a luna on horseback. (Hawai'i State Archives.)

Pictured here is a group of young Japanese women dressed for the fields, with a dog in the foreground. Note the machetes, ready for cutting cane. (Lyman Museum.)

As time went by, the Japanese immigrants adjusted to the new life and moved out of the plantations. Here, one young Japanese lady has made the transition and is pumping gas. (Lyman Museum.)

Pictured here are some Filipino workers, one carrying seed cane, probably in the 1920s. (Hawai'i State Archives.)

A Filipino worker proudly displays his son. In the early days of the sugar plantations, male workers were brought in alone, but in later years it was more common for the worker to bring his family. (Hawai'i State Archives.)

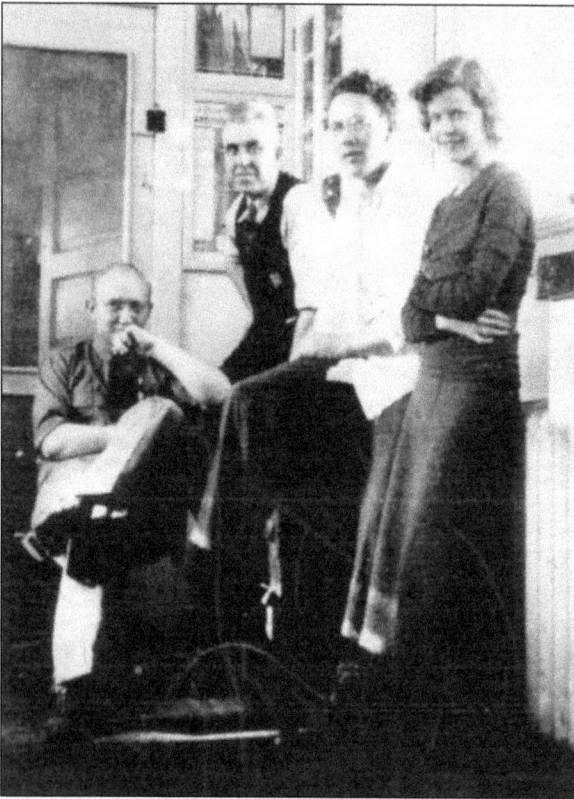

Caucasian haoles came to Hawai'i from the US mainland or even from Europe, mostly for managerial office work. This group worked for Hamakua Coast companies. (Ka'u Agribusiness.)

Housing for workers was sometimes rough in the early days, as in the case of this Japanese girl with a baby, probably in the 1890s. Worker housing improved substantially over the years. (Hawai'i State Archives.)

Pictured here is a typical row of houses built for plantation workers in Ka'u. Housing was provided in camps, often segregated by particular ethnic group. The plantation owners encouraged competition between the ethnic groups as a means of getting more from their workers. (Lyman Museum.)

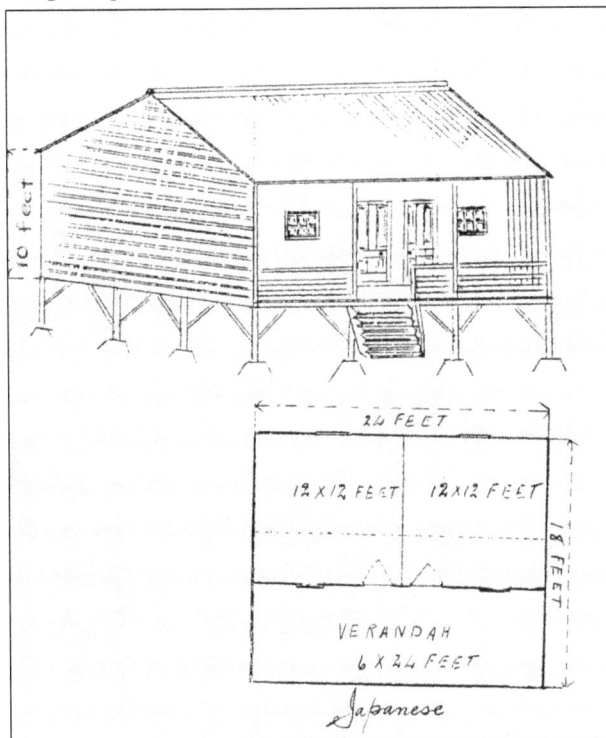

This is the plan of a house built around 1900 for two Japanese workers, with a 12-by-12-foot space plus lanai. Workers also had a patch of ground to grow their own vegetables. (Hawaiian Sugar Planters Association.)

A graduation event at a Japanese school is pictured. This photograph was taken around 1900. (Pahala Library.)

Shown is a kendo tournament in the 1930s on the grounds of a Japanese school. Sporting events were subsidized by the plantation owners to boost worker morale. (Pahala Library.)

Pictured is a big event hosted by the mill, with the county band playing, around 1926. Note the line of rail trucks carrying cane in the background on the left. (Hawai'i State Archives.)

Shown here is a line of people at a plantation event, another example of their popularity. This line is probably for food or scrip. (Pahala Library.)

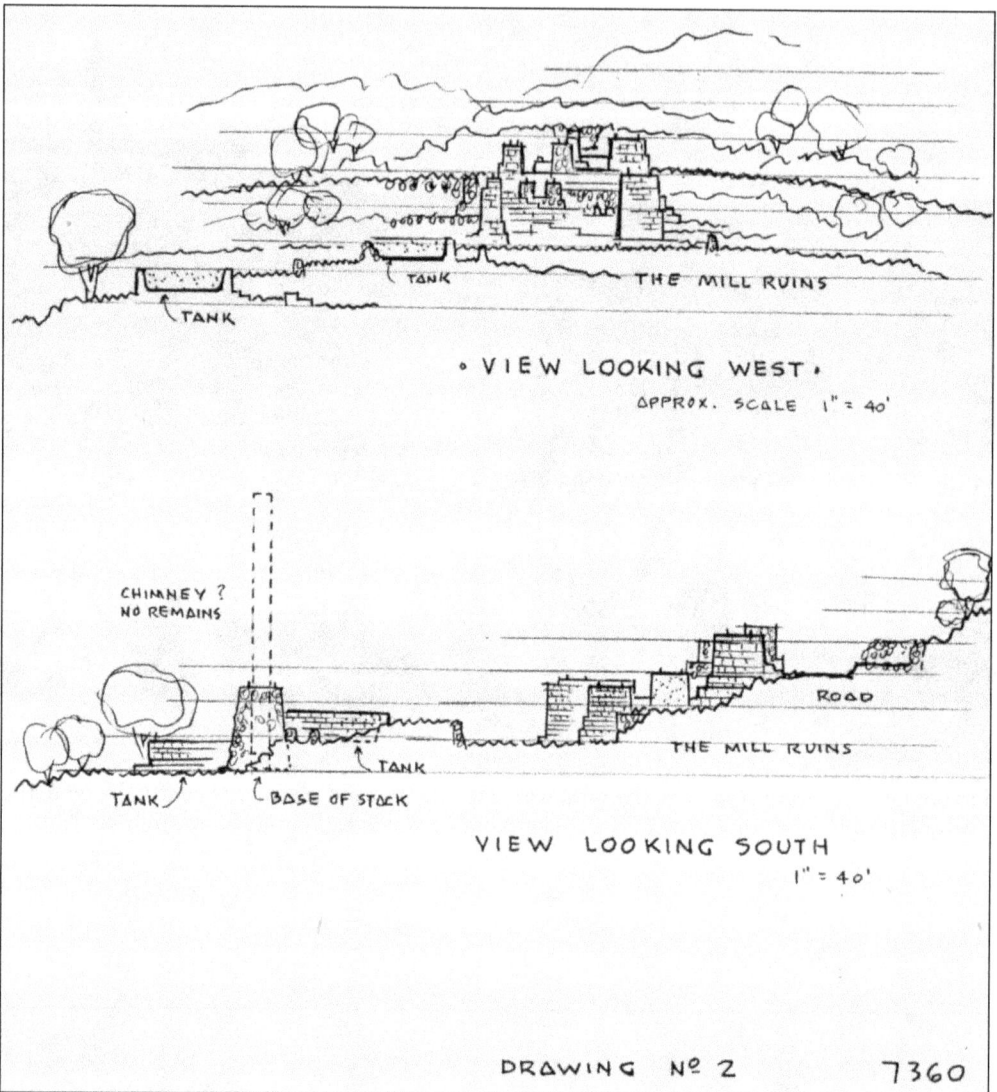

VIEW LOOKING WEST.

APPROX. SCALE 1" = 40'

TANK

TANK

THE MILL RUINS

CHIMNEY?
NO REMAINS

TANK

TANK

BASE OF STACK

ROAD

THE MILL RUINS

VIEW LOOKING SOUTH

1" = 40'

DRAWING Nº 2   7360

This is a 1973 rendition of the ruins of the Hilea Sugar Mill. The mill ruins are listed in the Hawai'i Register of Historic Places. (Hawai'i State Department of Land and Natural Resources.)

Three

WAIOHINU AND MARK TWAIN'S MONKEYPOD TREE

The name Wai'ohinu means "shining water," a name that has its origins in the reliable flow of water from the H'ao spring in the hills above. In 1866, the village was visited by Mark Twain, on a tour as correspondent for the *Sacramento Union* newspaper. Twain landed six miles away at Ka'alu'alu Bay and traveled on horseback to Waiohinu, where he stayed with Charles Spencer. He describes the scene as "green groves and flowers and occasional plains of grass." He was impressed with the fruit—mangoes, papayas, and bananas—but was disappointed that his favorite, cherimoya, was not in season. Since the land was favorable for agriculture, Waiohinu was where the sugar industry started in Ka'u, and the first mill was built there shortly before Twain's arrival.

One of the first missionaries, Rev. John D. Paris, arrived in 1841, and his house was one of the most notable victims of the earthquake that devastated the whole area in 1868. The beautiful fourth sanctuary of the Kauaha'ao Congregational Church was built in 1880, and Waiohinu was recognized as the district capital, designated as the county seat in 1900. There was a hotel, jail, post office, and school until the 1930s, when the sugar plantation owners focused their development on nearby Na'alehu, with the result that Waiohinu declined in relative importance. The plantation managers also redirected the spring so the only water that now flows through the village is in a drainage ditch. Visitors still stop to see the Mark Twain Tree, actually a descendant of the tree associated with the famous writer who wrote appreciatively about his stay in Waiohinu.

This Waiohinu mural was painted on the side of the Wong Yuen store by Pearl Maxner. The mural captures some highlights of the history of Waiohinu—the Ha'ao spring, the Mark Twain visit, the sugar industry, the Kauaha'ao Church, and some scenes from Hawaiian life. (Authors' collection.)

Waiohinu had its own "place of refuge," the Lua Nunu o Kamakalepo. The cave was excavated by William Bonk, and a few of the ornamental artifacts found are shown here: (a) a neck pendant (*niho palaoa*) of wood, (b) a pendant of pig tooth, (c, d) shell beads, (e) bead of conus shell, (f) bracelet plate of dog tooth, (i) bone awl, (j) bird bone-picker, and (k–n) bone needles. (*Archaeology in the Island of Hawai'i.*)

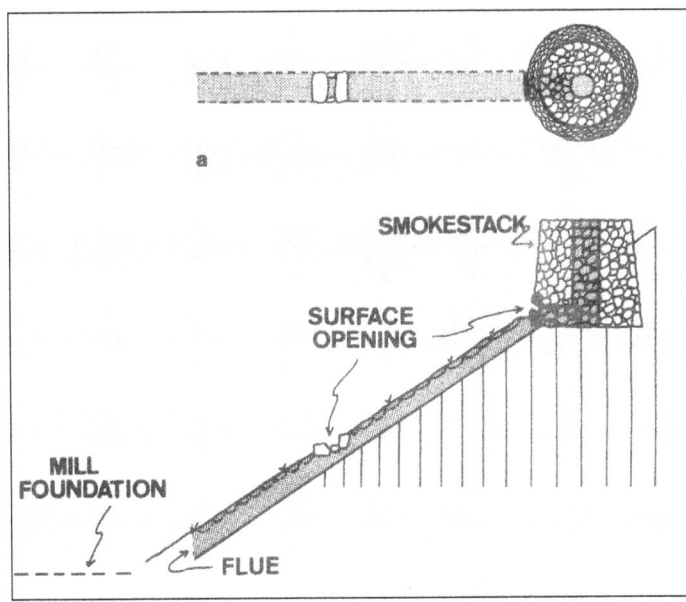

Pictured here is the arrangement in which the chimney flue of the first sugar mill in Kaʻu was laid around 1866 on the sloping hillside up to the smokestack. A vertical chimney was considered too risky because of the danger of earthquakes from Mauna Loa. ("Archaeological Survey and Excavations at Waiohinu Drainage Improvement Project, Kaʻu.")

Pictured here are the remains of the chimney of the first sugar mill in Kaʻu, located on the hillside above the Waiohinu Park. ("Archaeological Survey and Excavations at Waiohinu Drainage Improvement Project, Kaʻu.")

43

This is a drawing of Rev. John D. Paris's house before the earthquake. Reverend Paris was the first Congregational missionary in Ka'u, arriving in 1841. The house was totally destroyed by the earthquake of 1868, as were all the brick buildings in Waiohinu. (Mission Houses Museum Library.)

This photograph shows the ruins of the Catholic church in nearby Na'ohule'elua. The church was built in 1864 by the Sacred Heart Fathers from Belgium, a group that included Father Damien, now St. Damien. The church was fatally damaged in the great earthquake of 1868. (Authors' collection.)

Father Damien de Veuster was one of a group of Sacred Heart priests whose mission included Ka'u District. Together with a local carpenter, Damien built a rectory for his mentor Father Celestine Ruault. (Cardinal Wuerl's blog.)

Mark Twain, Waiohinu's most famous historical visitor, is pictured here in 1871. According to his own account, Twain did not really plant the Mark Twain Tree but stopped to talk to a group of local youths who were doing the planting. They invited him to hold one of the trees while they completed the planting. (Wikimedia Commons.)

Pictured here is the elegant fourth Kauaha'ao Congregational Church. The site was organized in 1841 by Rev. John D. Paris, the first Congregational minister in Ka'u. There were three simple churches that were used in the early years, but the church pictured here was built in 1880 under Rev. James Kauhane, the first Hawaiian minister. It was a simple white rectangular structure with green trim over the windows inside and out. The steeple was elaborate, with louvered sections and four pinnacles at the base of a simple spire. Inside were 28 pews and a very old organ, with kerosene lamps on the walls. The graveyard at the site has tombstones dating back to the 1800s. The photograph was taken in 1994, but the church was razed soon afterward because of dry rot and structural damage to the foundation. The demolition was highly controversial. (Jean Cooper.)

This photograph shows what is believed to be the first tractor in Waiohinu. It is pictured here about 1914 alongside two cars. (Lyman Museum.)

The Waiohinu Hotel is pictured here in 1913. (Lyman Museum.)

(ESTABLISHED 1872.)

C. MEINECKE,

General Merchant

And Postmaster,

WAIOHINU,

7 Miles from the Steamer Landing at Kaalualu,   Kau, Island of Hawaii.

Has much pleasure to have this opportunity to inform his friends on Hawaii and the public generally that he still carries on the above Store and Post Office, where is to be found an extensive assortment of all descriptions of

Dry Goods, Ready-Made Clothing, Groceries, Hardware,

Leather, Saddlery, Crockery, Cigars and Tobacco, Fancy Goods, Etc., Etc.

☞ Farmers, Planters and others will at all times receive at my Store FULL VALUE for their Coin.

This advertisement was placed by Charles Meineke for the post office and general store, established in 1872. Meineke was postmaster until 1900. In 1856, the local post office was designated Ka'u, with W.C. Shipman as its first postmaster. C.N. Spencer was postmaster from 1862 until 1866, but the office became Waiohinu in 1865. Nicholas George was postmaster for a short time in 1866, and he was followed by Thomas Martin, postmaster from 1868 to 1869. (Hawai'i State Archives.)

This is the house of William Meineke, Charles Meineke's grandson and a noted local historian. The house was built in the 1880s or 1890s and was one of few unaltered houses from that period until it was demolished in 1994. (Jean Cooper.)

Four

NA'ALEHU,
A PLANTATION TOWN

The name Na'alehu means "the volcanic ash," reflecting its location downwind from Kilauea volcano. Presumably, ash in the air was frequent at the time the name stuck, but today the volcano has reduced its output to vog, pollution that can be occasionally irritating. Na'alehu is a rather typical plantation town, with managers' houses along the highway and worker housing laid out above the town center, still called the Camp. The Camp is worth a visit during the evenings before Christmas, when the neighborhood has a tradition of outstanding Christmas lights.

Na'alehu became prominent as the sugar industry grew in the late 19th century. It had one of the largest mills anywhere and acquired public service buildings as the focus moved here from the former district capital in neighboring Waiohinu. Na'alehu has a post office, government building, library, and clinic. The population is only around 1,000 within the unofficial boundary, with a few thousand more living in the area around. Na'alehu has an amazing number of churches for a small community, reflecting its diverse population. The first immigrants were predominantly Japanese, but especially since World War II, most are Filipino. If a visitor hears a language other than English, it is likely not Japanese or Hawaiian but Ilocano, a language from Northern Luzon. Na'alehu's unique situation is its location as the southernmost community in the 50 states, so that it has the southernmost restaurant, farmers' market, and so forth, but it wears this distinction modestly, resisting the temptation to peddle aggressively "Southernmost" T-shirts.

In the plantation era, now gone, the plantation owners' approach was strongly paternalistic. They subsidized parades, the rodeo, a theater, and sporting events to help keep their workers happy. Many of these traditions are carried on today, especially the rodeo, which is still popular. The sugar industry has not been replaced, and there is a very strong resistance to change. Attempts to build a spaceport or a rehabilitation center, or even to upgrade the resort at nearby Sea Mountain, have met serious opposition, at least from a vocal minority. The future economy may depend mostly on agriculture but with more reliance on tourism, as more tourists come to appreciate a corner of relatively untouched Hawai'i.

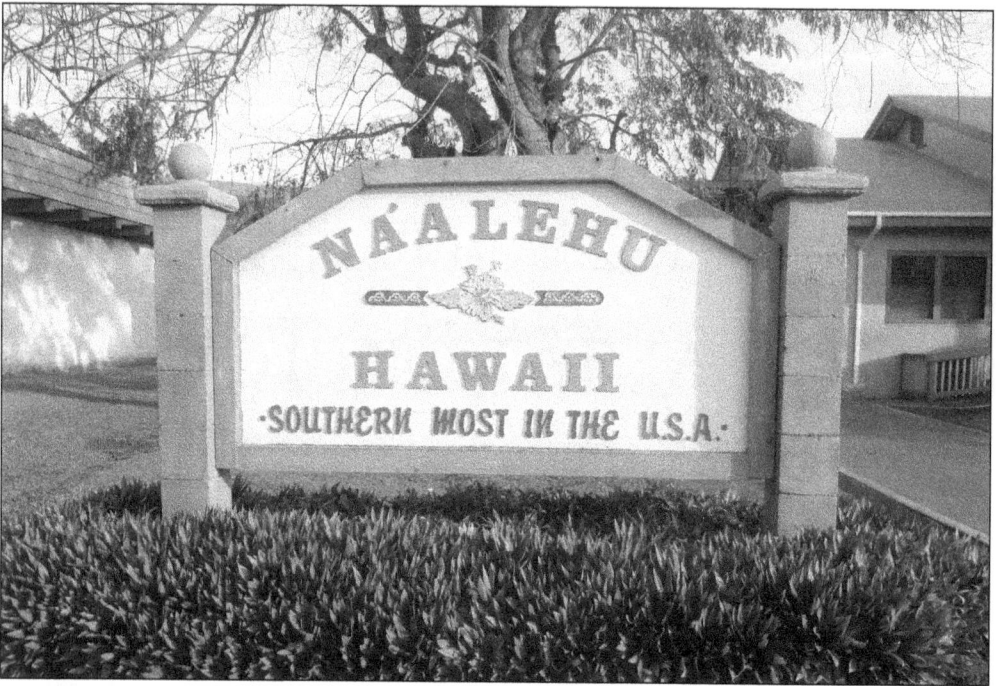

Naʻalehu is the southernmost community in the 50 states. The builder of the sign in this photograph was reluctant to claim Naʻalehu as a town or township, since, according to the dictionary, these have "certain local powers of government," which Naʻalehu does not. (Authors' collection.)

Pictured here is a pre-plantation dwelling made by Native Hawaiians in Naʻalehu. The timbers were cut in the forests and lashed together with coarse fibers from ʻukiʻuki or other plants. The thatching was usually of pili grass. A stone platform raised the floor above the earth and was covered with dry grass. (Hawaiʻi State Archives.)

Na'alehu's sugar mill was once one of the largest when it was built in 1870. The workers in front are drying sugarcane to make bagasse, which was used as a fuel and in buildings. The Na'alehu Theater has a ceiling and walls of made from bagasse. Few traces of the mill can now be seen, but parts were used in later buildings, such as Ka'u Auto Repair. (Hawai'i State Archives.)

This photograph features the safe from the Hutchinson Sugar Company, preserved and still used at the Ace Hardware Store in Na'alehu. (Authors' collection.)

In this photograph, taken about 1910, a plantation manager's house built along the highway is featured. (Sandy Sinclair.)

This photograph shows a group of workers returning home in the evening. (Lyman Museum.)

The plantation store, shown here, was demolished in 1969. The store was famous for exotic foods like chocolate-covered insects and small birds on skewers. (Hawai'i State Archives.)

Shown here are the buildings in the old center of Na'alehu. The structures pictured are, from left to right, the pool hall, dentist office, and Shimizu Hotel. This image was likely taken in the 1940s. On the right of the hotel was a garage and stables. (Photograph by Iwao Yonemitsu.)

The old Na'alelu theater, built by the plantation owners, is shown in this photograph. The movie being featured that night was *Murder on Campus*. The theater showed a Japanese film on Tuesdays, an X-rated film on Thursdays, and family movies on Saturdays. (Lyman Museum.)

Mules are passing through the center of Na'alehu, with the old theater in the background. Mules were the standard form of transport in the early stage of the sugar plantations. (Lyman Museum.)

Soldiers wait for transport to the mainland and possible service in World War I. Note that many are ethnic Japanese. (Iwao Yonemitsu.)

Pictured here is the first Buddhist temple in Naʻalehu, built in 1902 with funding from the plantation. Japanese immigrants brought Buddhism with them, and the temple became an important part of the immigrant community. The temple was built on land now used for parking. (Naʻalehu Hongwanji.)

This is the Odaisan Buddhist Temple in Naʻalehu, built around 1924. (Masako Sakata.)

This photograph shows members celebrating the 35th anniversary of the founding of the Na'alehu Hongwanji, in 1934. The temple had 134 members, pictured here outside the Japanese school. (Lyman Museum.)

This is the 1938 graduating class of Na'alehu Middle School. (Na'alehu Elementary and Intermediate School.)

Amy Fujimoto was queen in the 1948 Fourth of July parade. Na'alehu aimed to have the best Fourth of July parade on the island. (Iwao Yonemitsu.)

This 1948 photograph shows princesses riding in a convertible during a parade. (Iwao Yonemitsu.)

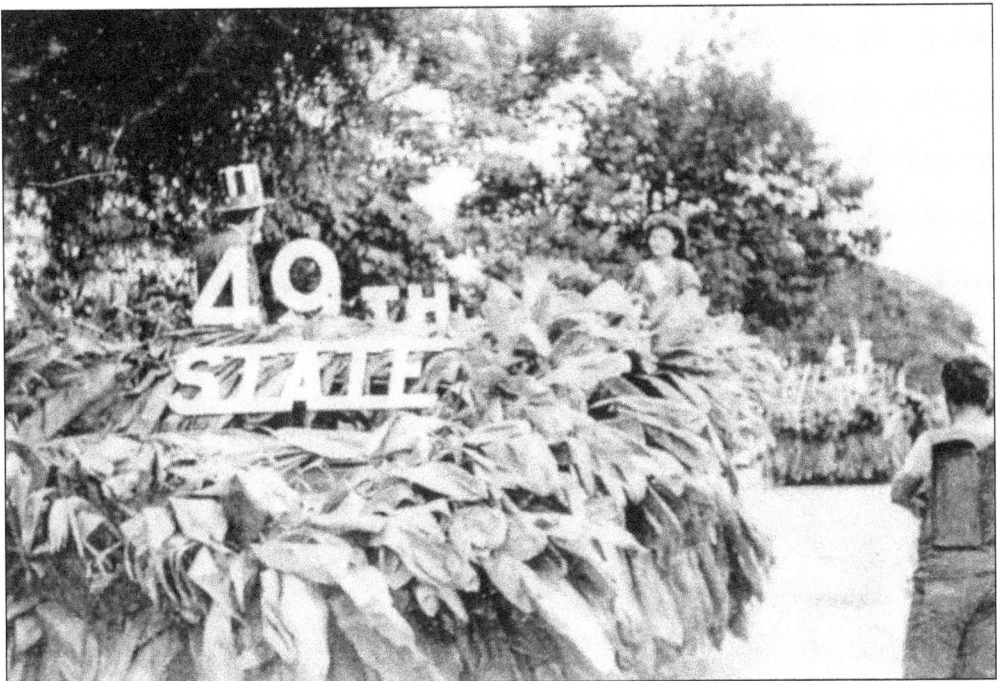

This is an image of a parade float waiting for the official designation of Hawai'i as the 49th state. Ultimately, Hawai'i would be the 50th, as Alaska's designation preceded it. (Iwao Yonemitsu.)

The float at left represents the Filipino community, the largest in Naʻalehu, at the 1948 Fourth of July Parade. The below image reflects the long-popular feature of horseback riders in the Fourth of July parade. (Both, Iwao Yonemitsu.)

Five

PAHALA AND THE END OF THE SUGAR INDUSTRY

The name Pahala is derived from the ancient practice of burning leaves of the *hala* plant to make a mulch to fill gaps in rocky volcanic soil. Pahala also gives its name to a type of soil—Pahala ash—that was deposited 13,000 to 30,000 years ago from Hawai'i's volcanoes. It is deepest near Pahala, up to 55 feet deep, and is fertile, making the area attractive for sugar planting. The first planters sent their cane to a mill in nearby Hilea, built in 1879, but work on Pahala's own mill began in 1880. This mill was second only to the Na'alehu Mill in size. The Hawaiian Sugar Company, based in Pahala, became the dominant force in Ka'u's sugar industry and in 1972 merged with Hutchinson Sugar to form Ka'u Sugar Company. The name was changed again in 1986 to Ka'u Agribusiness Company to reflect the expansion into macadamia nuts. As international competition got more severe, causing sugar industry recession all over Hawai'i, Ka'u Agribusiness closed down in 1996.

As the administrative center of the dominant sugar enterprise, Pahala became the location of Ka'u High School and Ka'u Hospital, and also the location of a branch of the Bank of Hawai'i. Once there were two gas stations in the main street, and the Chong Store was the largest retail outlet. Pahala was where the cowboys from Kapapala Ranch went to celebrate on Friday evenings. And it is the setting of *Saturday Night at the Pahala Theater*, by Lois-Ann Yamanaka, a raw collection of poems about growing up, mostly written in the local dialect. The book received the Pushcart Prize in 1993.

When the sugar industry closed, workers who had stayed were offered 15 acres for ranching or five acres for farming, on a free five-year lease. Most accepted the five-acre parcels and began the creation of the Ka'u coffee cooperative. Ka'u coffee is now winning state and international competitions, and its reputation for quality is well established, so coffee appears set to be the basis of the future economy of Pahala and its surroundings.

This photograph shows attendees at the Fourth of July fair enjoying the popular fair staple, the Ferris wheel. These attractions were in use for many years, and the Naʻalehu Fourth of July event attracted visitors from other islands, in addition to tourists. (Iwao Yonemitsu.)

The main street of Pahala had thriving businesses, including two gas stations, the Kanda Store, a barbershop, pool hall, beauty parlor, bank, and dentist's office. On the opposite side was a hotel and the Lee Chong store, which was the largest vendor in town. The post office was inside. (Pahala Library.)

This is the interior of the Lee Chong store. Note the hats in the display case. (Pahala Library.)

The merchants of the day, both in town and in the camps, liked to use tokens for as many purchases as they could and offered deals to persuade customers to use them rather than cash. The three tokens seen here are those of Ah Ling. (CGI.)

Pictured here is a lone boy playing in the street, with the Pahala theater in the background. The photograph was taken in 1972. (Franco Salmoiraghi.)

This photograph shows a graduation at Pahala School. Members of the first graduating class received their diplomas in 1940. (Iwao Yonemitsu.)

This two photographs document the changing fashion styles of Pahala youth. The photograph at left shows a group from 1972. The photograph below was taken in 1996, when the sugar industry closed. (Both, Franco Salmoiraghi.)

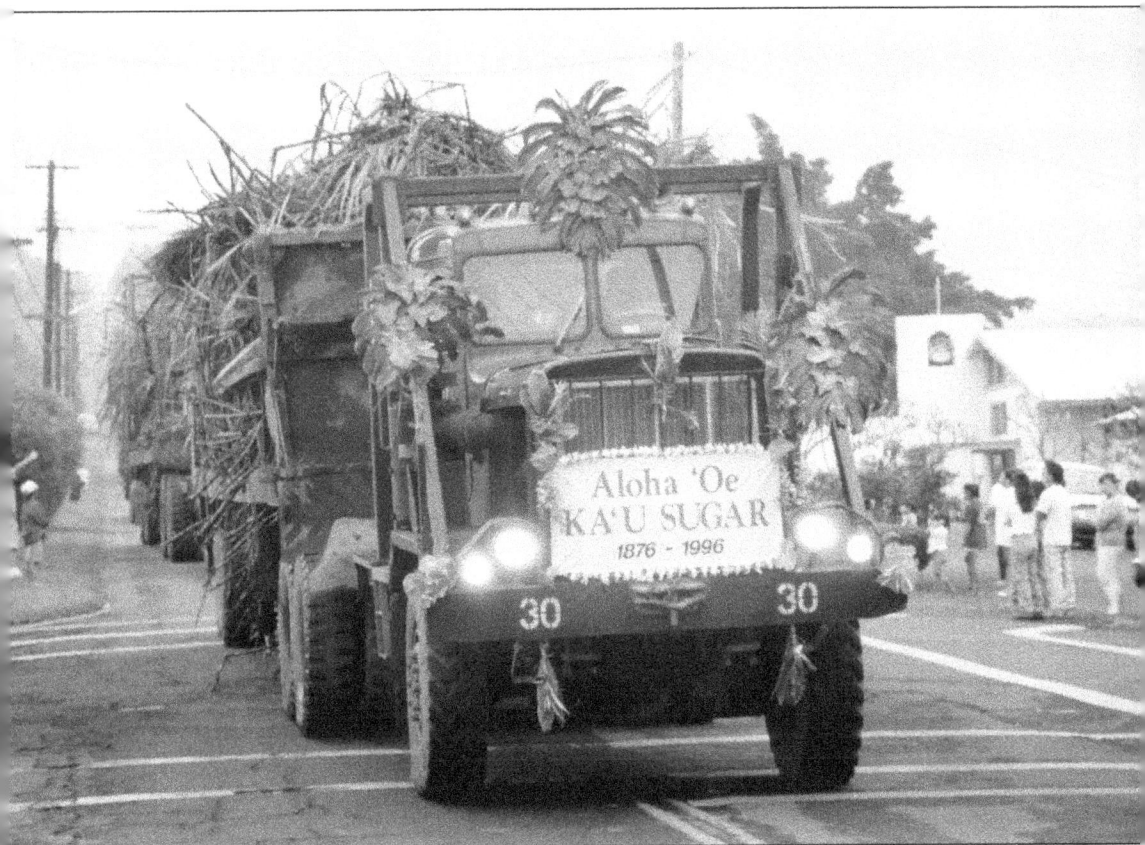

This is an image of the last truck carrying cane from the fields on the day of the final harvest, March 26, 1996. The truck was decorated, and the community gathered to witness this day that devastated the local economy and caused much suffering. (Franco Salmoiraghi.)

Driver Isidro Saribay stands by his truck decorated with sugarcane and ti leaves on the day the Pahala Mill closed. (Franco Salmoiraghi.)

Workers at the Pahala Mill are pictured here on the last day of operation in 1996. (Franco Salmoiraghi.)

This is an illustration of Ku-mauna, the Rain God of Ka'u, a rock formation above Hilea that collapsed after a rainstorm in the 1940s. (Authors' collection.)

The village of Hilea, between Pahala and Honu'apo, was once a thriving community. There were actually two villages, Hilea-uka, which was the original site, and Hilea-kai, close to the mill. The photograph shows that significant numbers of people were employed by the mill. (Sandy Sinclair.)

This is the manager's house in Hilea-kai with the mill in the background. (Sandy Sinclair.)

Aki's store in Hilea is pictured. The rider on the right was identified as Kainoakapuna. The man sitting on the left with a girl on his lap is Gil Patten. (Sandy Sinclair.)

The Spencer house in Hilea is pictured here around 1880. Standing on the left in the white dress is Annie Spencer, the wife of Charles N. Spencer. (Sandy Sinclair.)

Tibetan Buddhist temple Nechung Dorje Drayong Ling in Wood Valley was built in 1925, based on an original temple from 1902. The temple has been visited twice by the Dalai Lama, in 1980 and 1994. (Authors' collection.)

This is the Dalai Lama, leader in exile of Tibetan Buddhists. His second visit to the Wood Valley Temple was open to the public and attracted a crowd of around 3,500, with visitors from all over the world. (Buddhismus.)

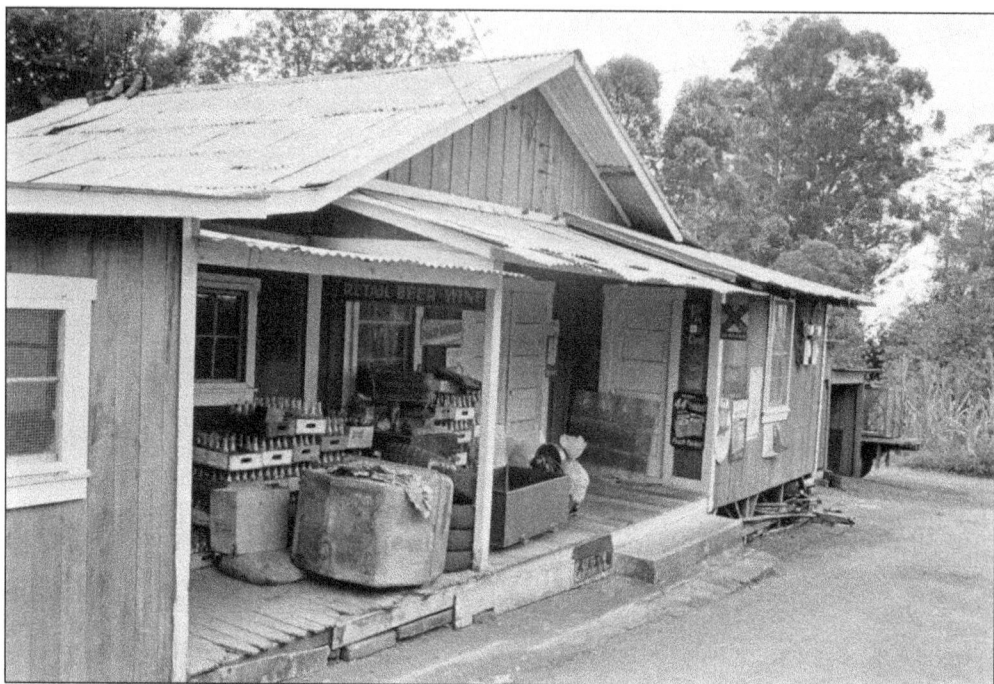

Shown here is the Wood Valley Camp Store. Wood Valley was the location of a number of independent sugar growers who sold cane to the plantation. It remains a quiet rural village, home of the well-known McCall's flowers. (Photograph by Franco Salmoiraghi.)

This local scene of a man and his dogs strolling down the lane in Wood Valley was captured by photographer Franco Salmoiraghi on the occasion of his visit to Ka'u to photograph the closure of the Pahala Sugar Mill. (Franco Salmoiraghi.)

Six

RANCHING AND THE PANIOLO IN KAʻU

Historically, ranching was the most important economic activity in Kaʻu after sugar. Ranching came to Hawaiʻi from Europe, the first cattle coming as a gift from Capt. George Vancouver to King Kamehameha in 1792. The first horses arrived in 1804. Both were new to Hawaiians and are explained to fellow Hawaiians by the historian David Malo in his book *Hawaiian Antiquities*: "The cow, a large animal with horns on its head; its flesh and milk are excellent food. The horse, a large animal. Men sit upon his back and ride; he has no horns on his head." Kamehameha declared a kapu (taboo) on killing the cattle, and the herds grew and roamed widely until the king hired a young ex-sailor, John Palmer Parker, in 1815, who began collecting the cattle and formed the nucleus of what eventually became Parker Ranch, once one of the largest in the world.

Since Hawaiʻi lacked workers with ranching experience, the first cowboys had to be brought in. Vaqueros were invited from Mexico around 1836 to teach the Hawaiians how to ride and to rope cattle. Hawaiians enjoyed the cowboy lifestyle, and the industry grew around the paniolo, or cowboy (the Hawaiian word is derived from the Spanish *español* [Spaniard]).

In Kaʻu, ranching developed strongly in the late 19th century. The first large ranch, Kapapala, was established in 1860 as a lease from Kamehameha IV to William Reed and Charles Richardson. The ranch grew in importance to provide support for the sugar plantation, providing meat and other supplies, and plantation owner Charles Brewer bought the property in 1877. Theophilus Brown bought the Kahuku Ranch in 1866, and his brother Robert was probably the first to run cattle there. His stay did not last long, as he was devastated by the great eruption of 1868 and moved soon afterwards, but the start there had been made.

Over the years, the industry has seen many changes, and ranch owners have struggled with profitability, but Kapapala Ranch still operates, and a few smaller ranches run cattle or horses throughout the district.

The cattle on Hawai'i's ranches were mostly Angus and a hybrid with Brahma known as Brangus. Initially, they were raised to provide beef for the plantations, but in recent times they are mostly used to produce calves that are shipped abroad for rearing in feedlots. (Lyman Museum.)

Horses were the main form of transportation around the ranches. In an interview, Paniolo Hall of Famer Tommy Kaniho said that a working cowboy could have as many as nine horses, with one in training. (Lyman Museum.)

Hawaiians loved to work as cowboys, and there was no shortage of applicants for ranching jobs once the original paniolo from Mexico had arrived to provide the training. Here, the photographer has captured the character of the tough, independent-minded Hawaiian paniolo. (Hawai'i State Archives.)

Here is another portrait of a Hawaiian paniolo, this one an older man, by outstanding artist Herb Kane. (Illustration by Herb Kawaaiunui Kane, from *Hawai'i Nei*.)

A key part of the working cowboy's set of tools is his saddle. This one from Kahuku Ranch is believed to have belonged to the last ranch manager, Earl Spence. The saddle shows Spanish influences. Below is a set of cowboy's tack hanging in what is likely Kahuku Ranch. (Both, Lyman Museum.)

This photograph shows roundup time. Long cattle drives were relatively rare, although at the time when Parker Ranch owned Kahuku Ranch, there were sometimes drives between the two. (Hawai'i State Archives.)

This is another photograph of a cattle drive. Gordon Cran of Kapapala Ranch recalled that most of the roundups in his experience were short, starting in the early morning and ending in the mid-afternoon. However, J.R. Molcilio, a Kahuku Ranch employee for 47 years, remembers some long drives from South Point. (Hawai'i State Archives.)

Before trucking became the norm, cattle were driven out to ships by first tying a few of them to small boats that were rowed out to the ship, where the cattle were hoisted aboard. Ka'alu'alu Bay was one location where Ka'u cattle were taken for shipping. (Hawai'i State Archives.)

Ranching at Kapapala began in 1860, when it was owned by the Hawaiian Agricultural Company to provide beef for the plantation workers. C. Brewer acquired the ranch in 1877 and operated it for 99 years, until it was bought by Parker Ranch, which wanted new acreage outside Waimea. (*Hawai'i Statehood Edition.*)

Gordon Cran was foreman at Kapapala and offered the ranch in 1997 at age 50. He raised the stock from 800 to 2,500 head on 30,000 acres and added small numbers of sheep, goats, and horses. (Jon Cran.)

Gordon Cran (1927–2007) was Hawaiian Cattleman of the Year 1995. He was survived by his wife, Jon. Kapapala Ranch is now run by Cran's daughter Lani and her husband, Bill Petrie. (Authors' collection.)

The first royal grant of part of what became Kahuku Ranch was in 1848 to ali'i William Pitt Leleihoku, who was governor of the island but died that year of measles. The photograph is of his grandson Prince Leleihoku, who became the owner in 1861 at age seven. He was a talented musician, very popular, and King Kalakaua named him as his heir. Unfortunately, the prince died from rheumatic fever in 1877 at the age of 23. (Hawai'i State Archives.)

Princess Ruth Ke'elikolani was wife of ali'i Leleihoku and foster mother of Prince Leleihoku. It is assumed that she managed the Kahuku property for most of the years when it was in royal hands. She became governess of Hawai'i Island after her husband's death and was said to be a very able administrator. (Hawai'i State Archives.)

Charles C. Harris served in many positions in the Hawaiian government, including attorney general and chief justice. He became owner of the Pakini Nui and Pakini Iki ahupua'a, part of what became Kahuku Ranch, by a royal patent of Kamehameha IV in 1861. A survey at that time recorded the size of Kahuku as 184,298 acres. (Hawai'i State Archives.)

In 1866, Kahuku was sold to Theophilus Brown, whose brother Robert was probably the first to run cattle there. Capt. Robert Brown was a former whaler and inventor of a harpoon gun. The photograph shows the Robert Brown family, including his wife, Charlotte, her brother John (on left), and six of their nine children. (Louise Prescott.)

Captain Brown was the unlucky rancher at the time of the great eruption of 1868. The family had to flee their collapsing house and find a hill to escape the lava flow. They left for Oʻahu soon afterwards and gave up the ranch. Captain Brown returned as an old man to look for the grave of his daughter Amanda, which had been buried by the lava flow. They were able to find the grave (shown here) and remove her body for reburial in a cemetery. (Lyman Museum.)

This is a roadside memorial erected for Captain Brown by a group of his descendants. The location is close to the site of the Browns' family house, but it is quite a distance from the 1868 lava flow. Captain Brown's descendants stay in touch and have regular reunions. (Authors' collection.)

In 1871, Kahuku Ranch was sold to George Jones and three partners whom he eventually bought out. The Jones years were the liveliest at Kahuku, in spite of another eruption of Mauna Loa in 1887. There were many parties, and guests included the lovely Princess Kaiulani, who stayed for a few days before leaving for school in England and her tragic death. (Hawai'i State Archives.)

Other guests at Kahuku Ranch in the Jones years included Charles Reed Bishop. He was the husband of Princess Bernice and served as minister of foreign affairs under King Lunalilo. A banker, Bishop was known as Hawai'i's greatest philanthropist. (Hawai'i State Archives.)

In 1888, Jones sold Kahuku to Samuel Norris, an eccentric who was known for his frequent legal battles. Norris was actually Danish, his real name Gotthilf Wilhelm Becher Christensen, and he made his fortune selling cattle to the military in California. He was 66 when he became a rancher in Hawai'i. (*Hawai'i . . . our New Possessions.*)

Unlike Jones, Norris was notorious for his inhospitality. This is recorded in a book, *Hawai'i . . . our New Possessions*, by John Musick, published in 1898. Musick describes a nightmare journey in fading light across rough lava after Norris turned him away one evening on the grounds that he "looked like a missionary." This drawing is from Musick's book. (*Hawai'i . . . our New Possessions.*)

In 1908, three paniolos from Parker Ranch entered the World Roping Championship in Cheyenne, Wyoming, and astonished the cowboy world by taking first, third, and sixth places in the steer-roping competition. They dressed differently from the cowboys of the Wild West and spoke a strange language—Hawaiian. Star of the Wyoming Championships was Ikua Purdy, whose 56 seconds easily broke the previous record. Purdy was the son of an Irish father and Hawaiian mother, and his achievement garnered national attention and inspired a number of songs about the Hawaiian cowboys. This statue commemorating Purdy's achievement is in Parker Ranch Center, Waimea. (Authors' collection.)

Freddy Rice was the manager responsible for a number of improvements to the ranch. Water was always a concern, and he enlarged the main reservoir to hold two million gallons and added a second reservoir. He also introduced a method of coating the lava with oil to reduce seepage. (Lyman Museum.)

Another of Rice's introductions was a Howe scale. Accurate weighing of the cattle was important in the struggle for profitability. Rice affirmed that he had increased the herd from an initial 700 to around 3,000. (Lyman Museum.)

The most radical of Freddy Rice's innovations was the introduction of bison in 1968. The American buffalo did not adapt well to the conditions in Kahuku. Mouflon sheep adapted better, and some survive in what is now the national park and elsewhere. Turkeys and pheasants that were part of the game reserve experiment also survived, and their descendants can sometimes be seen around Ka'u. (Lyman Museum.)

Shown is housing for the ranch workers. Housing was on two levels, with the upper level mostly for families. Electricity was provided by generators, just in the evenings. J.R. Molcilio said that when he was hired in 1952 at age 17, he was paid $50 a month and regular hands got $150, but the food and the life were good. (Lyman Museum.)

This is the gate of Kahuku Ranch. In 1997, the Damon Estates offered Kahuku Ranch, now a parcel of 117,678 acres, for sale. It took until 2003 for a buyer to appropriate enough funds for the purchase. (Lyman Museum.)

In 2003, the 116,000 acres of Kahuku Ranch were bought for $22 million by the National Park Service, with help from the Nature Conservancy (which put up the initial funds), to become the Kahuku Unit of Hawai'i Volcanoes National Park—increasing the size of the park by around 50 percent. Much of Ka'u District is located between the two segments of the national park. (Authors' collection.)

Seven

OCEAN VIEW AND THE
KULA KAI CAVERNS

Compared with the other communities in Kaʻu, Ocean View has a very recent history. In the late 1950s, the Damon Estates managers decided that the western end of Kahuku Ranch was too dry for economical cattle grazing so they sold off a large acreage. The Crawford Oil Company was the developer and created Hawaiian Ocean View Estates (HOVE), a subdivision of 10,697 one-acre lots extending from about 1,500 feet elevation to around 5,000 feet. It was believed to be the world's largest subdivision.

HOVE had 156 miles of roads, all of which were named by Lillian Crawford. With no county water, and electricity initially rare, HOVE attracted pioneering types, and a community entrepreneurial spirit has been carried down to the present day. One of the strengths of the Ocean View community has been its ability to create communal facilities with little or no help from county or state government. A community association was formed in 1969, and businesses started to open up in what are now three business centers mauka (toward the mountains) and makai (toward the ocean) of Highway 11.

The community of Ocean View now comprises Kahuku Country Gardens, Kula Kai View Estates, Kona Gardens, Keone's Ranchos, Kona South Estates, and Kona View Estates in addition to HOVE.

The Ocean View Business Association was formed in 1992, with Ken Arbo as its first president, and became Ocean View Chamber of Commerce, then later Kaʻu Chamber of Commerce. As early as 1993, the chamber published a directory of Kaʻu businesses that has been an important guide to local businesses and community resources. The 2015 directory lists 143 businesses and organizations.

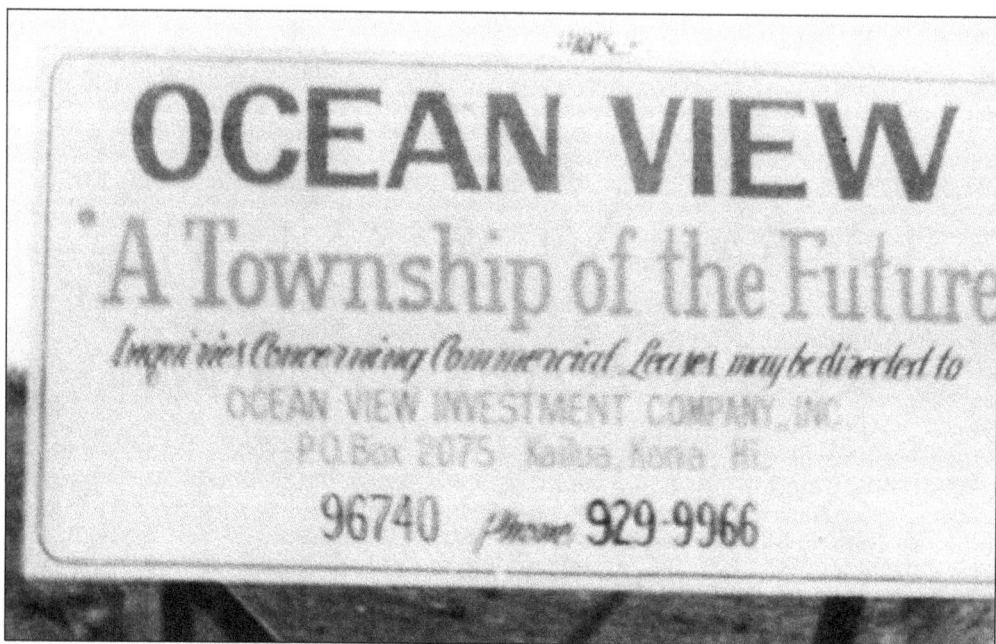

Ocean View was nicknamed "Township of the Future." This is one of the first real estate signs advertising the new township, probably in the late 1950s. Sales were originally handled out of the old Kona Inn Hotel. (Jim O'Hara.)

H. McKee was the leading realtor initially selling Ocean View Community Association (OVCA) lots. This image shows the house from which sales were conducted once the business was transferred from Kona. H. McKee Realty Inc. remains the most visible real estate office in Ocean View. (Sydney Sampson, H. McKee Realty.)

Pictured here is a typical road through Hawai'i Ocean View Estates in the early stages of development. In 1983, the trust fund set up by the developer was inadequate for maintenance, and the OVCA Road Maintenance Corporation was formed. It takes pride in keeping the 157 miles of private roads in good shape. (Jim O'Hara.)

Lava-rock surfaces are not the easiest for road construction. This photograph shows a log being removed on Sea Breeze. The engineer is Don Swangle. (Jim O'Hara.)

Above is the Ocean View Community Center under construction. Like the fire station, it was built entirely by volunteers. The photograph below shows some of the volunteers taking a break from the construction of the community center. (Both, Jim O'Hara.)

This mural in Ocean View features some typical Hawaiian activities, like poi pounding, tiki carving, and drystone wall building. In the background is Hawaiian sledding, *he'e holua*. This sport uses thin narrow sleds made from hardwoods, sliding down a prepared course. The sport is dangerous, as the sleds can reach speeds over 40 miles per hour. (Authors' collection.)

Ocean View's hidden gem is the Kula Kai Caverns, a system of lava tubes. When Mauna Loa erupts, it sends streams of lava down the slopes. The top of this hot lava flow is cooled by the air and may form a crust that acts as a roof for the lava that continues to flow below. Eventually, the lava flow stops, and the lava drains out, leaving a hollow tube. Formed from many generations of lava flows a 1,000 or so years ago, Kula Kai is part of one of the longest lava tube cave systems in the world (Kanohina System). Kula Kai is truly a treasure for cavers, with a variety of features to explore. A number of guided tours are available—from an easy walking tour to guided hard-hat tours with various levels of difficulty. In this photograph, a group of cavers gathers for a briefing, readying for the next part of the adventure. (Ric Elhard, Kula Kai Caverns.)

In this photograph, a group of cavers is shown dramatically outlined at the entrance to the Kula Kai Caverns. (Ric Elhard, Kula Kai Caverns.)

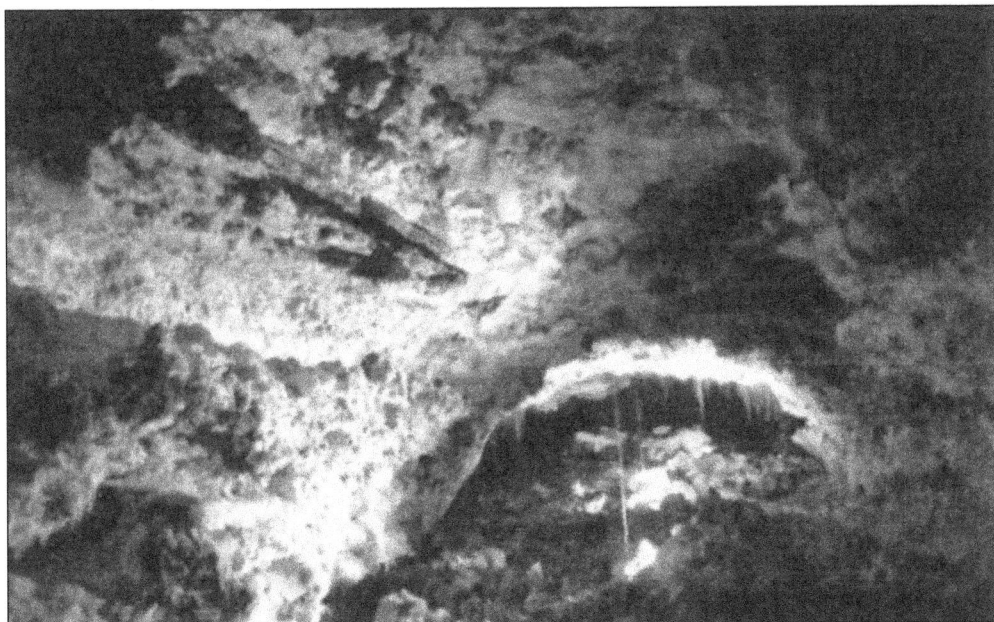

Since the lava tubes were formed so many years ago, they have had time to develop interesting formations on the walls. In this photograph, some fine stalactites can be seen. (Ric Elhard, Kula Kai Caverns.)

The lava tube caves were used for shelter and perhaps for longer-term occupation. In this section of Kula Kai, a historic shelter cave has been reconstructed for interpretation of the simple structures that were assembled for habitation. (Ric Elhard, Kula Kai Caverns.)

A close-up of the shelter cave shows a mat of dried grasses and vessels made from gourds. Stone tools found in the cave system can also be seen on close inspection. (Ric Elhard, Kula Kai Caverns.)

Eight

COASTAL KA'U, A HIDDEN TREASURE

The coastline of Ka'u is about 80 miles long, running from a nature reserve at Manuka Bay to Keauhou Point in Hawai'i Volcanoes National Park. The coastline is special because so much of it is unspoiled, the largest area of natural and undeveloped shoreline in the state of Hawai'i. Only about five miles of shoreline is accessible without four-wheel drive (or a boat). The coast is also a treasure trove of unique and endangered species, including the hawksbill turtle and the Hawaiian monk seal. There is only one resort, Sea Mountain at Punalu'u; however, much of the land is privately owned, so there is a real danger that more will be developed.

The historical importance of Coastal Ka'u—the likely landing place of the first Hawaiians, the battles for control of the island as a prelude to a united Hawaiian kingdom, and harbors for the sugar and ranching industries—is discussed in previous chapters. Ka'u also has the best collection of petroglyphs in the state at Pohue Bay. There are two state parks, at Honu'apo and Punalu'u, with good prospects for a third at Kawa Bay, generally regarded as the best surfing beach in Ka'u. Although Ka'u lacks a conventionally excellent white sand swimming beach, it is known for its "colorful" beaches. The black sand beach at Punalu'u is the best-known in the state, and there are several green sand beaches, the most popular being at Mahana Bay near South Point.

The pristine nature of so much Hawaiian coastline has drawn attention to the possibility that the coast of Ka'u be designated a national seashore or added to the Hawai'i Volcanoes National Park. A survey by the National Park Service concluded that the Ka'u coast contains cultural and historical resources of national importance. Many senators and representatives in Washington have expressed support for this idea. With much of Ka'u lying between the two units of the Hawai'i Volcanoes National Park, the designation of a national seashore would make Ka'u a true center for the appreciation of natural beauty. Already, the state highway winding around the southern slopes of Mauna Loa has been designated a Hawai'i State Scenic Byway, and plans for a hiking trail close to the shoreline, as part of the Ala Kahakai Trail, have been in the works for many years. Implementation of these three systems would create a trinity of opportunities to appreciate the spectacle of the Ka'u coastline.

Honuʻapo is the best harbor in Kaʻu and was clearly used in pre-contact times. Remains can be seen of a fishpond that was formed in the natural pond on the east side of the bay. As the sugar industry expanded, there was a need for a good harbor nearby both for bringing goods in and shipping sugar out. (Lyman Museum.)

In 1879, Alexander Hutchinson bought land at Honuʻapo for a harbor and mill. The mill was built soon afterwards. That same year, Hutchinson died in Honuʻapo Harbor in a strange accident while he was chasing indentured workers who were attempting to escape from their contract. (Hawaiʻi State Archives.)

This house on the Naʻalehu side of the harbor, with transport parked outside, is pictured sometime in the 1880s, with the mill in the background. At the time, Honuʻapo was a flourishing enterprise with warehouses and mill and rail connections. (Sandy Sinclair.)

This is the Honuʻapo landing in 1908. The pier at this stage is supported on trestles. The dories were used to transport loads from the pier to the coastal steamers that had to anchor in deeper water offshore. (Hawaiʻi State Archives.)

This photograph shows Honuʻapo in 1912. Bullocks were a useful source of power for heavy loads like stacks of sugarcane. And someone did have the latest form of personal transport. (Hawaiʻi State Archives.)

A new pier was built in 1910 at a cost of $13,482, jointly funded by Hutchinson Sugar, Inter-Island Steamship Company, and the Territory of Hawaiʻi. Trains could run right to the end for unloading of the pier, pictured here in 1917. Later, the end section of the pier was covered over. (Hawaiʻi State Archives.)

Well-wishers gather by the pier to give a send-off to troops on the start of their long journey to Europe to fight in World War I. This photograph was taken in 1917. (Lyman Museum.)

Shown here is a view of Honu'apo from the air in 1930. The covered section at the end of the pier can be seen on careful inspection. (Hawai'i State Archives.)

THE KAU BAZAAR

F. W. BARTELS,

General Merchant,

HONUAPO, KAU,   ISLAND OF HAWAII,

Has a full and general assortment of all kinds and descriptions of Dry Goods, Groceries, Hardware, Tinware, Crockery, Patent Medicines, Drugs, Boots and Shoes, Millinery, Cigars and Tobacco, Saddlery, Fancy Goods and Perfumery in great variety, at prices that will defy competition.

GIVE ME A CALL AND SEE FOR YOURSELVES.

I employ an *A No. 1 Cook*, and can supply Families and Tourists with all kinds of Cakes, etc. Wedding Cakes made a specialty. Also, various kinds of Confectionery.

Travelers and Tourists supplied with Good and Substantial Meals.

Honuʻapo village had a post office, Bartels Store, and the administrative center of the Kaʻu Bazar Sugar Company, later absorbed into Hutchinson Sugar Company. (Hawaiʻi State Archives.)

These bathing belles at Honuʻapo are standing near the rail tracks. (Iwao Yonemitsu.)

106

Honuʻapo means "the caught turtle," which most people assume to mean that the harbor is named from the old practice of catching turtles for eating. *Kupuna* Mabel Kaipo, with guidance from late local historian William Meineke, asserted she prefers the translation in which ʻapo means caught in the sense of "eyeballed," so the name came from observations of turtles as their heads bobbed up out of the water. The photograph shows a wedding in Honʻuapo, date unknown, with musicians. The prize exhibit is a turtle, which in this case is clearly the centerpiece of the wedding feast. This practice has since been banned. (Sandy Sinclair.)

Pictured here is flooding in Honuʻapo, probably at the time of the tsunami in 1946. This caused many businesses to close. The harbor was closed in 1942 as a precaution against invasion and never restored. There were tsunamis in 1960 and 1975. (Iwao Yonemitsu)

Punaluʻu was important historically as the headquarters of Keoua Kuʻahuʻula, the last aliʻi of Kaʻu. This mural of Keoua at Punaluʻu was painted by artist Herb Kane. As Kane was working on the mural, he had several visitors who told him their stories about Kaʻu. In his book *Pele: Goddess of Hawaii's Volcanoes*, Kane tells of his own strange experience. One evening, he was painting just by his work lights in a room he thought was locked, when an elderly Hawaiian woman appeared to him. He said "good evening," but she did not reply. Kane painted a few minutes more, then asked the security guard the identity of the old lady who was just there. The guard said, "What lady?" He had been there, but no one had come in or out. On a windy night about six weeks later, as the painting was nearing completion, Kane heard voices speaking Hawaiian. They seemed to be coming from the painting—from a group of chiefs painted standing on the beach. They were talking to each other! Then a lady in the left of the painting seemed to turn her head. Kane washed his brushes and went home. The next day, he looked at the mural and decided he could do no more. On the wall of the museum in Punaluʻu, the mural was, unfortunately, cut out and removed by thieves. (Authors' collection.)

Pictured here is the sacrificial stone located just outside the heiau called Halelau, or Kaeʻeleʻele, overlooking Punaluʻu Bay. (Bishop Museum.)

This is the Punalu'u landing in 1880. There was a small village with a Catholic church that can be seen in the distance as well as a school made of pili grass. The church was a victim of one of the tsunamis that hit the coast and caused the relocation of several coastal villages. (Hawai'i State Archives.)

Shown in this photograph is Punalu'u in 1890. The big house was presumably another structure damaged by the tsunami. (Lyman Museum.)

Punalu'u was used as a harbor for the sugar industry, but it was secondary to Honu'apo. Pictured here are sacks being unloaded, about 1915. (Hawai'i State Archives.)

Punalu'u had an elegant restaurant and bar overlooking the pond inland of the beach. There was a small but excellent museum where a mural (top of page 109) was located. The restaurant closed in the 1980s. (Authors' collection.)

Ninole Cove, on the south west side of Punalu'u, is the site of the Ka'ie'ie heiau, located on a promontory overlooking the bay. Close by, along an old government road, are a fishermen's shrine and the ruins of a school said to date back to the time of Kamehameha I. (Authors' collection.)

Punalu'u for most people is best known for its outstanding black sand beach and for the *honu*, the Pacific green turtle. (Photograph by Peter Anderson.)

In addition to having the best black sand beach in Hawai'i, Ka'u has the best green sand beach. It is in Mahana Bay, a couple of miles east of South Point. The green comes from tiny olivine crystals that form out of the lava; tidal action washes away less-dense grains, leaving a beach rich in olivine. (Photograph by Peter Anderson.)

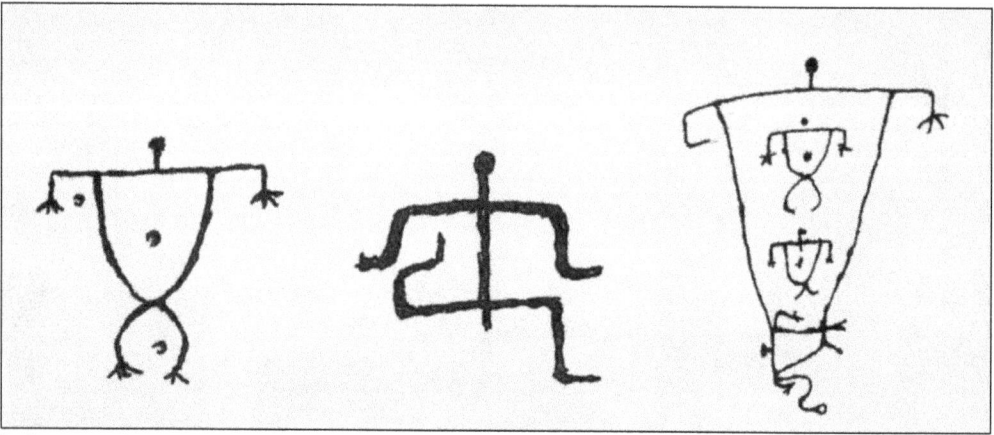

Pohue Bay has a large collection of petroglyphs. The examples shown here are, from left to right, a man, emphasizing the *pico* (navel); a runner; and a woman, emphasizing pregnancy and childbirth. (*Hawaiian Petroglyphs.*)

The Ka'u coast has some spectacular scenery. Perhaps the finest view is from South Point looking northwest along the cliffs. (Authors' collection.)

Nine

LIFE ON THE SLOPES
OF MAUNA LOA

Hawaiʻi sits over a geological hot spot where the earth's crust is thin, so that a reservoir of magma lies not too far from the surface. Mauna Loa, Kilauea, and especially the new volcano Loʻihi, still under the ocean, may erupt at any time. Fortunately, the eruptions are relatively gentle in comparison with the massive explosions, such as at Mount St. Helens, and rarely release highly toxic gases, such as at Pompeii. The relatively free-flowing lava creates a rounded mountain, so that Mauna Loa is designated a shield volcano.

Even if the volcanoes are relatively benign, they can still create havoc in the form of lava flows, earthquakes, vog, and tsunamis. The impact of previous eruptions has been felt throughout history, and examples are frequent. The great eruption of 1868 devastated Kaʻu District and caused the departure of Capt. Robert Brown, the first rancher at Kahuku. Tsunamis can be caused by eruptions either of Hawaiʻi's volcanoes or by distant eruptions around the Pacific, and they are more frequent than lava flows. This is one reason why Kaʻu has so few coastal settlements. Many villages used to be located along the coast but were abandoned after one of the many tsunamis.

The positive side of living on a volcano is that the eruptions have created a fascinating landscape with a rich variety of terrain, with vegetation depending on the age of the lava and the amount of local rainfall. The ongoing volcanic phenomena provide an opportunity to observe and study one of nature's wonders in relative safety, and Hawaiʻi Volcanoes National Park has become Hawaiʻi's prime tourist attraction, with 1,583,209 visitors in 2013. The national park, with the Kahuku unit now added to the main unit, is Kaʻu's unique treasure and there only because of the public's fascination with the wonders of Kilauea and Mauna Loa.

Lava fountains are the most spectacular features of eruptions. This one was generated in the 1949 eruption of Mauna Loa. (Hawai'i Volcanoes National Park.)

Kilauea's Halemaumau crater overflows as visitors stand nearby. (Hawai'i Volcanoes National Park.)

Four people walk on steaming *pahoehoe* lava. Pahoehoe is relatively smooth and unbroken, in contrast with *a'a*, which is made up of clustered individual rocks. Note that visitors would not be allowed to wander on hot steamy lava today. (Hawai'i Volcanoes National Park.)

Pictured here is the first Volcano House, built for the convenience of visitors to the Kilauea Crater. It was built in 1865 at the initiative of George Jones (sometime owner of Kahuku Ranch) and his partners Kaina, Charles, and Jules Richardson. (Hawai'i State Archives.)

This photograph shows a group of ladies enjoying the fireside at the Volcano House on a cool evening, around 1895. (Hawai'i Volcanoes National Park.)

Horseback provided an alternative way of viewing the volcanoes. There was a trail; otherwise, traveling on pahoehoe lava can be tricky. (Hawai'i State Archives.)

A party of visitors departs from Punalu'u on its way to visit Kilauea. The first visitors to write about their visit to the volcano were the English missionary William Ellis and the American Asa Thurston in 1823. (Hawaiian Historical Society, photograph by J.J. Williams.)

A group of visitors traipses in the fern forest with a ranger, date unknown. The man in the background, probably a bird-watcher, has binoculars. (Hawai'i Volcanoes National Park.)

Another form of transport is shown here. It looks like there are three or four cars on this road to the national park around 1923. (Hawai'i State Archives.)

This group of early visitors appears to be cooking something. Rather than food, what they actually have on the ends of the sticks are postcards. The idea was to char the outside of the postcard a little, then mail it to friends as evidence that one was up close with some hot lava. This kind of access to the lava and activity could be dangerous and would not be allowed today. The photograph was used for some time on colorized postcards that were sold in the gift shop. (Hawai'i Volcanoes National Park.)

Thomas Jagger was the first scientist to undertake serious long-term study in Hawai'i Volcanoes National Park. He founded the Hawai'i Volcanoes Observatory, where a museum is now named in his honor. Jagger is on the extreme right of the back row of this group, wearing his uniform. (Hawai'i Volcanoes National Park.)

Pres. Franklin D. Roosevelt is pictured here at the rim of Halemaumau Crater in 1934. Roosevelt is in the car, wearing a hat and sitting upright. (Library of Congress.)

Large numbers of native species have become extinct because of competition from invasive species or the onslaught of animals like feral pigs. The national park provides protection for threatened species like the Ka'u silversword. (Bill Doar.)

This is a close-up of the silversword's flower spike, with 30 to 600 disc-shaped florets, which are purple, red, or yellow in color. The Ka'u silversword grows best in moist locations between 5,000 and 8,000 feet in elevation. (Bill Doar.)

Conservation is an important role for the national park. One of its prime responsibilities is the preservation of the nene, or Hawaiian goose, Hawai'i's state bird. (Lyman Museum.)

Visitors are often surprised to find a military camp inside the national park. The Kilauea Military Camp was originally a training camp, but it is now a recreational venue for active military and veterans. The photograph shows the entire complement turning out on a wet day in 1948 to give a farewell salute to Gen. James Ware, on his retirement as commanding officer. (Hawai'i Volcanoes National Park.)

BIBLIOGRAPHY

Bonk, William J. *Archaeology in the Island of Hawai'i*. Honolulu: University of Hawai'i, 1969.

Cahill, Emmett. *The Dark Decade 1829–1839*. Honolulu: Mutual Publishing, 2004.

Cordy, Ross. *Exalted Sits the Chief*. Honolulu: Mutual Publishing, 2000.

Cox, J.H. and E. Stasack. *Hawaiian Petroglyphs*. Honolulu: Bishop Museum, 1988.

Dorrance, William H. and Francis S. Morgan. *Sugar Islands*. Honolulu: Mutual Publishing, 2000.

Handy, E.S. Craighill and Mary Kawena Pukui. *The Polynesian Family System in Ka'u Hawai'i*. Honolulu: Mutual Publishing, 1998.

Kane, Herb. *Pele: Goddess of Hawaii's Volcanoes*. Captain Cook, HI: Kawainui Press, 1987.

Kelly, M. and S.N. Crozier, "Archaeological Survey and Excavations at Waiohinu Drainage Improvement Project, Ka'u," Bishop Museum, 1972.

Kelly, Marion. "Historical Background of the South Point Area, Ka'u, Hawai'i," *Pacific Anthropological Records* 6 (1969).

———. *Majestic Ka'u, Mo'olelo of Nine Ahupua'a*. Honolulu: Bishop Museum, 1980.

Kirch, Patrick V. *Feathered Gods and Fishhooks*. Honolulu: University of Hawai'i Press, 1985.

Malo, David. *Hawaiian Antiquities*. Translated by N.S. Emerson. London: Forgotten Books, 2013. First published 1903.

Musick, John R. *Hawai'i . . . our New Possessions*. New York: Funk & Wagnalls, 1898.

Sinoto, Y. and M. Kelly. "Archaeological and Historical Survey of Pakini-nui and Pakini-iki Coastal Sites," Bishop Museum, 1975.

Tabrah, Ruth. *Hawai'i Nei*. Chicago: Follett, 1968.

Takaki, Ronald. *Pau Hana*. Honolulu: University of Hawai'i Press, 1983.

Visit us at
arcadiapublishing.com